Current Issues
and the
Study of Ancient History

Publications of the
Association of Ancient Historians

The purpose of the monograph series is to survey the state of the current scholarship in various areas of ancient history.

#1 Past and Future in Ancient History
    Chester G. Starr

#2 The Shifting Sands of History: Interpretations of Ptolemaic Egypt
    Alan E. Samuel

#3 Roman Imperial Grand Strategy
    Arther Ferrill

#4 Myth Becomes History: Pre-Classical Greece
    Carol G. Thomas

#5 Ancient History: Recent Work and New Directions
    Stanley M. Burstein, Ramsay MacMullen, Kurt A. Raaflaub, and Allen M. Ward

#6 Before Alexander: Constructing Early Macedonia
    Eugene N. Borza

Other publications by the Association

Makedonika: Essays by Eugene N. Borza
Edited by Carol G. Thomas

The Coming of The Greeks
James T. Hooker

Directory of Ancient Historians in the United States, 2nd ed.
Compiled by Konrad Kinzl

Current Issues and the Study of Ancient History

Publications of the
Association of
Ancient Historians 7

Stanley M. Burstein
Nancy Demand
Ian Morris
Lawrence Tritle

 Regina Books
Claremont, California

Library of Congress Cataloging-in-Publication Data

Current issues and the study of ancient history / Stanley M. Burstein...
   [et al.].p. cm. -- (Publications of the Association of Ancient
   Historians; 7)
Rev. papers originally presented in a joint AAH/AHA (Association of
   Ancient Historians/American Historical Association) session at the
   Annual Meeting of the American Historical Association in Jan.
   2000. "Co-published by arrangement with the Association of
   Ancient Historians"--T.p. verso.
   Includes bibliographical references.
   ISBN 1-930053-10-X (alk. paper)
   1.   History,   Ancient--Historiography--Congresses.   2.   Blacks—
   Historiography--Congresses.   3.   Africa--Civilization--Western
   influences. 4. History--Philosophy--Congresses. 5. Afrocentrism--
   Philosophy--Congresses. 6. Eurocentrism--Congresses. 7. Greece--
   Civilization--Congresses.   I.   Burstein,   Stanley   Mayer.   II.
   Association of Ancient Historians. III. American Historical
   Association. IV. Series.
   D80 .C87 2002
   930'.07'2--dc21

                                                    2002003657

Co-published by arrangement with the
Association of Ancient Historians

Regina Books

Post Office Box 280
Claremont, California 91711
Tel: (909) 624-8466 / Fax (909) 626-1345

Manufactured in the United States of America.

CONTENTS

PREFACE

The seventh pamphlet in the publication series of the Association of Ancient Historians continues the goal of the series: to further the teaching and study of ancient history through succinct accounts describing basic directions in the field. Narrative is accompanied by bibliographic references to aid further investigation of the subject. The theme of this volume–*Current Issues and the Study of Ancient History*–offers an overview of the impact of four approaches to the study of antiquity that have gained adherence in recent years.

Following the pattern of PAAH 5–*Ancient History: Recent Work and New Directions*–this volume brings together essays of four scholars who are respected experts in specific approaches to ancient history: ethnicity, gender studies, archaeological theory and psychological history. Stanley M. Burstein, Professor of History at California State University/Los Angeles, uses the issue of Afrocentrism and the Greeks to examine the influence of ethnicity in studying antiquity. Professor of History at the University of Indiana Nancy Demand considers recent contributions of gender studies to the field of ancient history. Archaeology and ancient Greek social history are the twin foci of Ian Morris, Professor of Ancient History and Archaeology at Stanford University. Lawrence Tritle, Professor of History at Loyola Marymount University, looks inward to the psyche in his reflections on the link between psychology and history. His elegant paper demonstrates that Thucydides' experience in the Peloponnesian War and that of participants in the war in Vietnam provide many common insights into human reactions under stress.

Akin to PAAH5, these essays also had a preview. They were presented in a joint AAH/AHA session at the annual meeting of the American Historical Association in January 2000. In addition to the four presenters, Eugene Borza, Professor Emeritus, Pennsylvania State University, offered a commentary. Since an aim of our society is to make the presence and value of ancient history visible to colleagues in other fields, we were pleased by the size of the audience (more than ninety people) and its interest. A friend who read a draft of these works commented that the scope of these essays "once again reinforces the overwhelmingly cross-disciplinary nature of historical discourse at present whether it be psychological, ethnic- or gender-based or simply a reevaluation of archaeological theory."*

In concluding his remarks, Professor Borza stated his view that "To judge by these papers it would appear that the study of Greek and Roman history in this country is healthy, marked by honest scholarship, a wide diversity of methods, and characterized by attempts to look at the past in refreshing new ways." It is our hope that readers of these revised essays will come to a similar conclusion.

Carol Thomas
Past President of the AAH
Organizer of the AAH/AHA session

---

* Wallace Mead, to whom thanks is due for bringing uniformity to the formats of these essays.

I

A CONTESTED HISTORY:
EGYPT, GREECE AND AFROCENTRISM*

Stanley M. Burstein

Debates among ancient historians rarely are "news". Yet for much of the past decade discussion of a relatively esoteric subject, the relationship between the civilizations of ancient Egypt and Greece, has been "news". Three of the principal American professional organizations concerned with antiquity—the American Philological Association, the American Research Center in Egypt, and the American Historical Association—all devoted special sessions at their annual meetings to the subject. Major scholarly journals organized "virtual sessions" in print by devoting whole issues or large sections of issues to consideration of the topic and its ramifications.

Even more remarkable, the topic engaged the interest of the commercial media and the general public. Numerous articles appeared in newspapers, many with emotionally charged titles such as: "Out of Egypt, Greece", "The African Origins of 'Western Civ'" and "Not Out of Africa"—the title also of a well-known book on the subject by Professor Mary Lefkowitz.[1] It was the subject of television shows and even a "rap" song. An e-mail bulletin board sponsored by the publisher of *Not Out of Africa* in the spring of 1996 attracted more than 2,600 subscribers

---

*An earlier version of this paper was published under the title "Egypt and Greece: Afrocentrism and Greek History," *Were the Achievements of Ancient Greece Borrowed from Africa?* (Washington, D.C. 1997). Reprinted by permission of the Society for the Preservation of the Greek Heritage.

[1] Mary Lefkowitz, *Not Out of Africa: How Afrocentrism Became an Excuse to Teach Myth as History*, 2nd. ed. (New York 1997).

during its short existence. Quite unexpectedly, Greek history and Greek historians were drafted into the so-called "Culture Wars".[2]

The impetus for this remarkable surge of interest in what might be called the " Ancient Egyptian question" is clear. It was the publication in 1987 of the first volume of *Black Athena: The Afro-Asiatic Roots of Classical Civilization*.[3] A second volume[4] has since appeared, and the sensation it created in "the Academy" is only now showing signs of abating, so that it is appropriate to try to step back and to assess the overall character and significance of this long and contentious debate.

Black Athena is the work of Martin Bernal, a respected historian of Communist China and Professor of Government at Cornell University; and, as even a cursory glance at its contents will confirm, it is hardly the sort of book that one would expect to become the center of a furious public controversy. As the first volume's subtitle—*The Fabrication of Ancient Greece 1785-1985*—indicates, it is a detailed almost 500 page long critical analysis of the writing of Greek history during the last two centuries. Hardly the typical best seller! And, indeed, interest in *Black Athena* was slow to develop outside the United States.[5]

---

[2]The controversy is comprehensively reviewed in Jacques Berlinerblau, *Heresy in the University: The Black Athena Controversy and the Reponsibility of American Intellectuals* (New Brunswick 1999). For an Afrocentric view of the issues involved see Molefi Kete Asante, *The Painful Demise of Eurocentrism: An Afrocentric Response to Critics* (Trenton 1999).

[3]Martin Bernal, *Black Athena: The Afro-Asiatic Roots of Classical Civilization, Volume I: The Fabrication of Ancient Greece 1785-1985* (London 1987).

[4]Martin Bernal, *Black Athena: The Afroasiatic Roots of Classical Civilization, Volume II: The Archaeological and Documentary Evidence* (London 1991).

[5]This may be changing. Italian, German, French, Spanish, Swedish, and French translations of *Black Athena* have now appeared. The Dutch Classical journal *Talanta* has devoted a whole volume to *Black Athena-Black Athena: Ten Years After*, edited by Wim M. J. van Binsbergen, *Talanta* 28-29 (1996-1997); while the whole topic of Afrocentrism and its connection to Black Athena is reviewed in Francois-Xavier Fauvell-Aymar, Jean-Pierre Chrétien, and Claude-Hélène Perrot, eds., *Afrocentrismes: L'histoire des Africains entre Égypte et Amérique* (Paris 2000).

In scholarship like so much else, however, topicality and timing are all important, and *Black Athena* was both topical and timely. *Black Athena* is an exhaustive and, at times, exhausting, critique of modern historians of ancient Greece that appeared at a time when Multiculturalism and Post-modernist criticism of the academic disciplines had become major issues in humanistic scholarship. Unlike so many works of contemporary scholarship in the Humanities, Professor Bernal presented his critique clearly and forcefully and left no doubt that in his opinion the stakes were unusually high: nothing less than our entire understanding of the origins of Greek and Western civilization.

The core of Professor Bernal's critique of recent Greek historiography consists of three points. First, ancient Greek writers claimed that important elements of Greek civilization had been borrowed from the ancient civilizations of the Near East and especially Egypt during the second millennium BC when Greece had been colonized by Egyptians and Phoenicians. Second, evidence of this colonization was preserved in two sources: Greek myths and legend and ancient Greek itself, almost forty percent of whose vocabulary Professor Bernal claims consists of foreign loan words, primarily of Semitic and Egyptian origin. Third, this view of Greek history, which Professor Bernal calls the "Ancient Model", was accepted without question by scholars until the nineteenth century when it was suddenly replaced by the "Aryan Model" which assigned sole credit for the creation of Greek civilization to white invaders from northern Europe and Central Asia.

Professor Bernal is also equally clear and forthright about the reason for the replacement of the "Ancient Model" by the "Aryan Model". It was not, he maintains, the result of the progress of "objective" scholarship but of racist and nationalist prejudice. Nineteenth century European historians—especially British and German historians—could not accept that the Greeks, whom they idealized, owed anything to the ancestors of the dark skinned peoples their countries were busy conquering. For this reason he argues that future progress in the understanding of Greek history is possible only if contemporary Greek historians follow the lead of the ancient Greeks and again put the "Ancient Model" with its emphasis on Egypt and the Near East at the center of Greek historical studies.

Black Athena understandably created a sensation among Classicists and Greek historians. No critique of Classics and Greek historiography on this scale had ever appeared before.

Black Athena is also a remarkably fascinating work to read. It combines the titillation of a tabloid expose of the sins of the founding fathers of contemporary Greek historiography with an uncompromising denunciation of everything we teach our students about Greek history and how it should be studied. The passage of time, however, has brought perspective. Professor Bernal's goals for *Black Athena* were ambitious: to lessen European cultural arrogance and to provide a new framework for the study of Greek history. Although his project is only half-complete—volumes on the linguistic and mythical evidence for his thesis are yet to come—it is increasingly clear that neither goal is likely to be achieved.

The publication of the first two volumes of *Black Athena* sparked an unprecedented outpouring of articles and reviews. The most important of these studies are now conveniently collected in the volume *Black Athena Revisited* edited by Mary Lefkowitz and Guy Rogers.[6] Even a cursory reading of these studies leaves no doubt that, while Professor Bernal's critique of 18th and especially 19th century Greek historiography has considerable merit, the flaws in *Black Athena* are too numerous and significant for it to serve either as a secure guide to the history of Greek historiography or as a framework for the future study of Greek history. Books, however, have their own fates. The intended audience for *Black Athena* was Classicists and Greek historians, and it clearly reached that audience. But it also found an enthusiastic reception from African American intellectuals. The reasons for this development, which Professor Bernal does not seem to have anticipated, are to be found in events of the late 1980s.

The late 1980s saw efforts in various American cities with large African American populations to introduce into the public schools what were called "Afrocentric" curricula. The most controversial and influential of these curricula was developed by the Portland Oregon School District and distributed throughout the United States in a volume of essays entitled *African-American*

---

[6]Mary Lefkowitz and Guy MacLean Rogers, eds., *Black Athena Revisited* (Chapel Hill 1996). Professor Bernal has now responded to the criticisms in these articles in Martin Bernal, *Black Athena Writes Back: Martin Bernal Responds to his Critics* (Durham 2001).

Baseline Essays.[7] One of the principal goals of such reforms was, in the words of a 1990 District of Columbia school district task force report,[8] to place at the center of the Black educational experience "Ancient African history that is the foundation of World Civilization" and "classical African thought which impressively influenced the Hellenic world, early Christianity, Judaism and later the European Renaissance". Attempts to implement such reforms could and did provoke fierce controversy. In California the city of Oakland rejected the state approved Social Studies textbooks and even attempted to write its own.[9] It is hardly surprising, therefore, that supporters of Afrocentric curricula welcomed the support that *Black Athena* and its sensational expose of the "racist and nationalist" roots of academic Greek history could provide their cause.

The almost simultaneous controversies over the adoption of Afrocentric curricula in the public schools and *Black Athena* had an unexpected result. Greek historians and the mainstream media simultaneously became aware of the existence among African American intellectuals of an alternative Afrocentric version of Greek history that, like *Black Athena*, emphasized the central importance of Egypt in the history of Greece and through Greece that of Western Civilization as a whole. The general thrust of this reconstruction of Greek history is summed up in the titles of two of the most famous works of Afrocentric historiography: *Africa: Mother of Western Civilization* by Yosef A. A. ben-Jochannan[10] and *Stolen Legacy: Greek Philosophy is Stolen Egyptian Philosophy* by George G. M. James.[11]

Because Egypt and not Greece is at the heart of Afrocentric discourse, extended discussions of Greek history by Afrocentrists are comparatively rare. Indeed, *Stolen Legacy: Greek Philosophy*

---

[7]Cf. Eric Martel, "Teacher's Corner: Ancient Africa and the Portland Curriculum Resource," *Anthro Notes* 13,2 (Spring, 1991) 7-10.

[8]*Superintendent's African-Centered Education Initiative, Task Force Report,* Washington D.C. (October, 1990) 10.

[9]The Oakland textbook controversy is described in Todd Gitlin, *The Twilight of Common Dreams: Why America is Wracked by Culture Wars* (New York 1995) 7-32.

[10]Yosef A. A. ben-Johannan, *Africa: Mother of Western Civilization* (New York 1971).

[11]George G. M. James, *Stolen Legacy: Greek Philosophy is Stolen Egyptian Philosophy* (New York 1954).

is Stolen Egyptian Philosophy is one of the few full length Afrocentrist studies of any aspect of Greek history.[12] It is not surprising, therefore, that Afrocentric discussions of Greek history are largely limited to one topic: contact between Greece and Egypt and its effects. Five main themes recur in these discussions: first, ancient Egyptians would be considered Blacks according to definitions of that term that have been traditionally used in the United States; second, Egypt was the first and most influential ancient civilization; third, Greeks became civilized by appropriating Egyptian learning; fourth, many important figures in Greek history including the mathematician Euclid, and, of course, the Ptolemaic queen Cleopatra VII were Blacks; and fifth, evidence supporting these claims exists in classical literature but has been suppressed by Eurocentric white historians. The most influential force shaping contemporary Afrocentrist discussion of these issues has been the work of the Senegalese scholar Cheik Anta Diop.[13]

Cheik Anta Diop is best known outside Afrocentrist circles for his insistence that Egypt was a "Black civilization" and his melodramatic suggestion that Egyptologists conspired to suppress this fact by hiding or destroying black mummies. In actuality, however, he was a philosopher of history in the tradition of Oswald Spengler and Arnold Toynbee, who articulated a view of world history of remarkable comprehensiveness in which the relationship between Egypt and Greece plays a critical role.[14] Educated at the Sorbonne under the distinguished Greek historian André Aymard at the time of the dissolution of France's African empire in the 1950s, Diop devoted his considerable scholarly

---

[12]Cf. Dr. Henry Olela, *From Ancient Africa to Ancient Greece: An Introduction to the History of Philosophy* (Atlanta 1981).

[13]For the influence of Cheik Anta Diop on contemporary Afrocentric thought, see Wilson Jeremiah Moses, *Afrotopia: The Roots of African American Popular History* (Cambridge 1998) 223-225.

[14]For Diop's views on Greek history see especially Cheik Anta Diop, *The African Origin of Civilization: Myth or Reality* (Westport 1974); *Precolonial Black Africa: A Comparative Study of the Political and Social Systems of Europe and Black Africa, From Antiquity to the Formation of Modern States* (Westport 1987); *The Cultural Unity of Black Africa* (London 1989); and *Civilization or Barbarism: An Authentic Anthropology* (Westport 1991). A sympathetic study of Diop and his school is Chris Grey, *Conceptions of History: Cheik Anta Diop & Theophile Obenga* (London 1989).

ability to developing an interpretation of African history that would simultaneously affirm the autonomy of African culture and its significance in world history.

According to that interpretation, the history of civilization in the Old World took the form of a Manichaean conflict between the peoples of what Diop called the two "cradles": a harsh northern cradle located in the steppes of Central Asia and led by the Greeks and a benign and creative southern cradle in Egypt whence civilization originated and spread throughout the Mediterranean basin and the Near East. The histories of the two cradles first intersected in the second millennium BC when Greek invaders overwhelmed the "African" Minoans, thereby, beginning a process of "White" aggression against the southern cradle that has continued up to the present. Before their ultimate defeat, however, the representatives of the southern cradle succeeded in civilizing their Greek conquerors. Thereafter, at critical junctures in Greek history Greek culture was reinvigorated by renewed contact with the Egyptian sources of its culture, first by Greek intellectuals who came to study in Egypt and then by the wholesale appropriation of Egyptian culture by Greeks following the conquest of Egypt by Alexander the Great in the fourth century BC.

Diop's vision is a tragic one, a nightmare history from which he urged Africans to awake and renew their culture by returning to their Egyptian roots and making Egypt play the same role in African education and culture that Athens and Greece do in Western culture. Unlike George G. M. James, however, Diop recognized the originality of Greek culture and its world historical significance, but he denied it positive value, claiming that the savage central Asian environment in which the Greeks originated rendered them incapable of understanding the spiritual dimension of the Egyptian roots of their civilization. In Diop's words, "the Greeks merely continued and developed, sometimes partially, what the Egyptians had invented. By virtue of their materialistic tendencies, the Greeks stripped those inventions of the religious, idealistic shell in which the Egyptians had enveloped them."[15] In

---

[15]Diop's thesis has been fleshed out in Jacob H. Carruthers, *Mdu Ntr Divine Speech: A Historiographical Reflection of African Deep Thought from the Time of Pharaohs to the Present* (London 1995); and Molefi Kete Asante, *The Egyptian Philosophers: Ancient African Voices from Imhotep to Akhenaton* (Chicago 2000).

other words, which is positive in the Greek achievement is traceable to its Egyptian roots, what is negative to its Greek roots; and that contradiction is the ultimate cause of the recurrent crises that have wracked Western Civilization up to the present.

The initial encounter with the Afrocentric version of Greek history is disconcerting. Part of the problem is style. Afrocentric Greek historiography is polemical in character and deliberately provocative in tone; the use of the word "stolen" to characterize the relationship of Greek philosophy to Egyptian thought is an obvious example. More disturbing, however, are three characteristic features of this literature: its pervasive concern for race as a determinant of ethnicity and culture, its reliance on outdated scholarship, and its repeated and uncritical citation of a handful of ancient proof texts to support hypotheses such as the supposed existence of an "Egyptian mystery system" which is claimed to have been the source of most early Greek philosophy. Especially unsettling is the tendency of Afrocentrists to dismiss all criticism by non-Afrocentrist scholars as simply the result of the critic writing within a Eurocentric and/or racist framework.

Understandably, the first response of most Greek historians upon reading such works is the desire to dismiss them as "bad history" and to get on with doing real "Greek History". Yielding to that temptation would, however, be a mistake for two reasons. First, our students, as the Egyptologist Ann Macy Roth[16] recently noted, read these works; and it behooves us to be able to respond intelligently to their questions, and, second, the issues they raise are important and central to any understanding of Greek history. Equally misguided, I believe, is the tendency to dismiss Afrocentric ancient history as simply a "myth" or the creation of intellectual charlatans perpetrating a fraud on the African American community and its students.

Afrocentric historians are numerous and varied. They include amateur enthusiasts and academics, who hold Ph.D.s from major universities and teach in various university departments. They hold their own conferences, have research institutes devoted to their studies, and publish the results of their research in their own

---

[16]Ann Macy Roth, "Building Bridges to Afrocentrism: A Letter to My Egyptological Colleagues," *American Research Center in Egypt Newsletter* 167 (September, 1995) 1, 14-17; 168 (December, 1995) 1, 12-15.

journals.[17] The expansion in the volume of and audience for Afrocentric ancient history is, in fact, one of the many results of a major development in recent American social history: the emergence of a growing college educated African American middle class with a strong interest in Africa and African culture. The recent burgeoning of Afrocentric history has, however, misled the media and many critics of Afrocentrism into believing that Afrocentric historiography itself is also a recent phenomenon.[18] In actuality, the Afrocentric approach to ancient history is almost two hundred years old and has deep roots in African American intellectual history.

The origins of Afrocentric ancient history are to be found in the now almost forgotten, but bitter, nineteenth century debate over the capacity of the Negro for civilization.[19] This debate was part of the greater conflict over the abolition of slavery and the future role of freed slaves in America and was conducted with understandable intensity. At its heart was a simple question: could Blacks survive and function as freemen in civilized society? Not surprisingly, its participants stated their cases in the starkest possible terms. At the core of the negative case were the twin claims that Blacks had never created a civilization and that Africa had no history. So, Commander Andrew H. Foote asserted in *Africa and the American Flag*—an account of the early years of Liberia—that "if all that negroes of all generations have ever done were to be obliterated from recollection forever, the world would lose no great truth, no profitable art, no exemplary form of life. The loss of all that is African would offer no memorable deduction from anything but the earth's black catalogue of crimes."[20]

---

[17]Most notably *The Journal of African Civilizations* and *The Journal of Black Studies*.

[18]This is a common theme in the articles collected in John J. Miller, ed., *Alternatives to Afrocentrism* (Washington, D.C. 1994).

[19]For this debate see William Stanton, *The Leopards Spots: Scientific Attitudes toward Race in America 1815-59* (Chicago 1960); and David S. Wiesen, "Herodotus and the Modern Debate Over Race and Slavery," *The Ancient World* 3 (1980) 3-16.

[20]Andrew H. Foote, *Africa and the American Flag* (New York: D. Appleton & Co. 1854). 206-207. The passage occurs in the context of a passage denying Africans any role in Roman history. Cf. Edward W. Blyden,

Some of the participants in this debate went further and ascribed separate origins to Blacks and Whites. Among the most important supporters of this extreme position was the American consul in Cairo, George Gliddon. Today, Gliddon is probably best known as one of the protagonists in Edgar Allen Poe's witty science fiction tale, "Some Words with a Mummy." In the mid-19th century, however, his reputation rested on two other achievements: his 1842 Lowell Lectures which, published under the title *Ancient Egypt*,[21] introduced modern Egyptology to literate America and his collaboration with the famous Philadelphia doctor and "craniologist" Samuel Morton. By using his Egyptological expertise to undermine the authority of the classical accounts of Egypt on the one hand and his Egyptian connections to provide Morton with genuine ancient Egyptian skulls for analysis on the other,[22] Gliddon earned the distinction of being, according to his admirers, the person who "was the first to announce that Egyptians were caucasians and not blacks."[23]

This unfortunate alliance of early Egyptology and physical anthropology with 19th century racism helped engender a mistrust of mainstream ancient scholarship on the part of some African and African American intellectuals that continues to the present.[24] Equally unfortunate was the important and invidious role Greece and Greek culture played in this debate. As Thomas Jefferson's and John C. Calhoun's notorious rhetorical promises

---

"The Negro in Ancient History," *The People of Africa*, ed. by Henry M. Schieffelin (New York 1871) 1-2.

[21]George Gliddon, *Ancient Egypt* (Philadelphia 1850). My copy describes itself as the "fifteenth" edition.

[22] For Gliddon's contribution to Samuel G. Morton, *Crania Aegyptiaca; or Observations on Egyptian Ethnography, Derived from Anatomy, History and the Monuments* (Philadelphia 1844), see William Stanton (n.19) 45-53. Bernal curiously ignores the significance of Gliddon and his colleagues for development of the idea of the Egyptians as Caucasians; cf. Robert Young, "Egypt in America: Black Athena, Racism and Colonial Discourse," *Racism, Modernity and Identity On the Western Front*, edited by Ali Rattansi and Sallie Westwood (Cambridge 1994) 150-169.

[23]Editor, "A Sketch of the Progress of Archaeological Science in America," *The Southern Literary Messenger* 11(1845) 427.

[24]E.g. the rejection of Champollion's decipherment of hieroglyphics by Martin R. Delany, *The Origin of Races and Color* (Philadelphia 1879; rpr. Baltimore 1991) 47-51.

to reconsider their views on Negro inferiority if Blacks could be shown to be "capable of tracing and comprehending the investigations of Euclid"[25] or conjugating a Greek verb indicated, Greek culture was held up as the absolute standard by which the extent and quality of Black achievement or failure was to be judged.[26]

Blacks in the early United States and elsewhere responded to these challenges in three ways. Some, such as the Philadelphia doctor and polymath Martin R. Delany, denied the findings of the new Egyptology on which their supporters relied. Others tried to meet them "head-on" and, like the printer and inventor Benjamin Banneker in the eighteenth century and the educator and missionary Alexander Crummell in the nineteenth century, actually took up the challenge and mastered the intricacies of Euclidean geometry and the Greek verb. Indeed, in her autobiography written in 1913 the Philadelphia educator Fanny Jackson Coppin still remembered how she had felt that she "had the honor of the whole African race on my shoulders" during her Greek recitations at Oberlin College after the Civil War.[27] More numerous and influential, however, were those who chose the third path and sought to vindicate "the Moral, Intellectual, and Religious Capabilities of the Coloured Portion of the Mankind"[28] by turning the tables on their opponents and claiming a major role for Africans in the origins of civilization in general and of Greek civilization in particular. Specifically, they

---

[25]Thomas Jefferson, *Notes on Virginia*, Query XIV.

[26]Alexander Crummell, "The Attitude of the American Mind toward the Negro Intellect," *Destiny and Race: Selected Writings 1840-1898*, edited by Wilson Jeremiah Moses (Amherst 1992) 292. For this theme in general, see Henry Louis Gates, Jr., "Authority, (White) Power, and the (Black) Critic; or, it's all Greek to me," *The Future of Literary Theory*, ed. by Ralph Cohen (London 1989) 324-346.

[27]Fanny Jackson Coppin, *Reminiscences of School Life, and Hints on Teaching*, edited by Shelley P. Haley (New York 1955) 15; Coppin refers to Calhoun's challenge twice in her memoir (pp. 19 and 30). Cf. Halley, xxii-xxiv.

[28]Part of the title of a book by Wilson Armistead, *A Tribute for the Negro: Being a Vindication of the Moral, Intellectual, and Religious Capabilities of the Coloured Portion of Mankind: with Particular Reference to the African Race* (1848).

maintained that civilization originated in Ethiopia and reached Greece through the mediation of Egypt.

The argument had roots in Biblical and ancient Greek thought,[29] and was one of the strongest arrows in the quiver of early advocates of the equality and humanity of blacks. So, the French writer Henri Grégoire[30] incorporated it into a trenchant critique of Thomas Jefferson's notorious disparaging remarks concerning Blacks in *The Notes on Virginia*.[31] And it continued to be cited for this purpose by opponents of slavery such as the economist and critic of colonization, Alexander Everett,[32] and the abolitionist, Lydia Maria Child.[33] The earliest examples of the use of the theme by Black writers date from the 1820s and the 1830s, and it became a characteristic feature of nineteenth century Black historical writing in the United States and elsewhere thereafter. Examples are numerous[34] and include pamphlets, public speeches, scholarly articles, school textbooks, and even an adventure novel published in 1903 by the African American novelist Pauline E. Hopkins in which an African American explorer discovers near the ruins of Meroe living descendants of

---

[29]The key texts are *Psalms* 68: 31 and Diodorus 3.2-3.

[30]Henri Grégoire, *An Enquiry Concerning the Intellectual and Moral Faculties, and Literature of Negroes*, trans. David Bailie Warden (1810), ed. by Graham Russell Hodges (Armonk 1997).

[31]Thomas Jefferson, *Notes on Virginia*, Query XIV.

[32]Alexander H. Everett, *America or A General Survey of the Political Situation of the Several Powers of the Western Continent with Conjectures on their Future Prospects* (Philadelphia 1827) 213-219.

[33]L. Maria Child, *An Appeal in Favor of Americans Called Africans* (New York 1836) 148-151, 168-176.

[34]An excellent anthology of such texts is *Classical Black Nationalism: From the American Revolution to Marcus Garvey*, edited by Wilson Jeremiah Moses (New York 1996). For an illuminating recent overview, see Mia Bay, *The White Image in the Black Mind: African American Ideas about White People, 1830-1925* (New York 2000). This approach was not limited to African-American writers but was a standard feature also of early abolitionist polemics; cf. George M. Fredrickson, *The Black Image in the White Mind: The Debate on Afro-American Character and Destiny, 1817-1914* (New York 1971) 13-15. For an interpretation of this tradition more sympathetic to Afrocentrism see Maghan Keita, *Race and the Writing of History: Riddling the Sphinx* (Oxford 2000).

the ancient Ethiopians, who were the creators of civilization.[35] The clearest and most elegant statement of the theme, however, was provided not by an American but by the distinguished Anglo-African scientist and scholar, James Africanus Beale Horton, who wrote in his 1868 book, *West African Countries and Peoples and A Vindication of the African Race*, that:[36]

> Africa, in ages past, was the nursery of science and literature; from thence they were taught in Greece and Rome, so that it was said that the ancient Greeks represented their favourite goddess of Wisdom —Minerva—as an African princess. Pilgrimages were made to Africa in search of knowledge by such men as Solon, Plato, Pythagoras; and several came to listen to the instruction of the African Euclid, who was at the head of the most celebrated mathematical school in the world, and who flourished 300 years before the birth of Christ....Many eminent writers and historians agree that these ancient Ethiopians were Negroes, but many deny that this was the case. The accounts given by Herodotus, who traveled in Egypt, and other writers settle the question that they were. Herodotus describes them [sc. the Ethiopians] as '*woolly-haired blacks with projecting lips*'.[37] In describing the people of Colchis, he says that they were Egyptian colonists, who were '*black in complexion and woolly-haired*'. This description undoubtedly refers to a race of Negroes....Say not, then...that Africa is without her heraldry of science and fame. Its inhabitants are the offshoots...of a stem which was once proudly luxuriant in the fruits of learning and taste; whilst that from which the Goths, their calumniators have sprung, remained hard, and knotted, and barren.

Bridge players call this trumping your opponent, and anyone who has ever played bridge can understand the attraction of this argument, especially since it could be extremely effective because

---

[35]Cf. Dickson D. Bruce, Jr., "Ancient Africa and the Early Black American Historians, 1883-1915," *American Quarterly* 36 (1984) 685-699; and Clarence Walker, *Deromanticizing Black History: Critical Essays and Reappraisals* (Knoxville 1991) 87-94. A more general and fuller critical history of Afrocentrism is Stephen Howe, *Afrocentrism: Mythical Pasts and Imagined Homes* (London 1998). Pauline E. Hopkins' novel, *Of One Blood. Or, the Hidden Self*, is reprinted in *The Magazine Novels of Pauline Hopkins*, edited by Hazel Canby (New York 1988) 441-621.

[36]James Africanus Horton, *West African Countries and Peoples 1868*, with an introduction by George Shepperson (Edinburgh 1969) 59-60. I have omitted Horton's references to Roman and early Christian history.

[37]Horton is probably quoting from memory since Herodotus does describe Aithiopians as "woolly-haired (7.70)" but not with "projecting lips."

both Black and White participants in the debate shared essentially the same classical education. So, for example, while testifying before the U.S. Senate in 1883, Richard Wright, the founder of Savannah State College, responded to a question about the "comparative inferiority and superiority of races" by observing that "the majority of the sciences…have come from the colored races…, that the Egyptians were actually woolly-haired negroes…," and that the "same thing is stated in Herodotus, and in a number of other authors with whom you gentlemen (sc. the Senators) are doubtless familiar."[38]

The problem is not the truth or falsity of the arguments presented in these passages and many others like them, but the fact that they could easily appear without significant change in almost any contemporary Afrocentric study of the relationship between Egypt and Greece. Put simply, Afrocentric ancient history with its trust in the literal meaning of "authoritative" texts and its reliance on diffusion as the principal explanation for cultural change is not so much bad history as old fashioned history. As the distinguished African philosopher Kwame Anthony Appiah perceptively noted, what is most striking about Afrocentric history is "how thoroughly at home it is in the frameworks of nineteenth century European thought".[39] The irony is that Afrocentrists continue to fight with nineteenth century weapons—their arguments clearly reflect Bernal's "Ancient Model"—a nineteenth century battle, whose principal objectives were achieved long ago. So, no reputable historian today doubts that Africa has a long and important history or that Egypt was the creation of Africans or, most important, that Egypt exercised significant influence on the development of Greek civilization.[40] So much for the past; what about the present and future?

---

[38]My italics. Wright's testimony is quoted in James D. Anderson, *The Education of Blacks in the South, 1860-1935* (Chapel Hill 1988) 29-30.

[39]Kwame Anthony Appiah, "Europe Upside Down: Fallacies of the new Afrocentrism," *(London) Times Literary Supplement* (February 12, 1993) 24.

[40]By the end of the nineteenth century Egyptologists largely accepted the African character of Egyptian civilization, but tried to evade the obvious implications of that position by identifying the Egyptians as "Hamites"— Brown caucasians—and not "Negroes"; cf. Wyatt MacGaffey, "Concepts of Race in the Historiography of Northeast Africa," *Journal of African History* 7 (1966) 1-17; and Howe (n.35) 115-121for good discussions of the Hamite

As I already mentioned, one of the main contentions of Afrocentrist scholars is that Greek historians have attempted to suppress all evidence of relations between Egypt and Greece and the significant influence Egypt exercised on the formation of Greek civilization. The truth is just the opposite. Relations between Greece and Egypt have always interested Greek historians, and in recent years their study has become one of the most active and dynamic areas of Greek historical studies as new discoveries have transformed our understanding of the extent and significance of contact with Egypt in Greek history.[41]

Most dramatically affected have been our ideas concerning relations between the Aegean and Egypt during the second millennium BC. The fact of Aegean contact with and influence from Egypt during the Middle and Late Bronze Ages—roughly the seventeenth through the fourteenth centuries BC—has been known since the beginning of Minoan and Mycenaean studies in the late nineteenth century. By the beginning of the twentieth century scholars could cite a wealth of iconographic, artifactual, textual, and linguistic evidence including: the use of Egyptian conventions, themes, and techniques in Minoan art; the adoption of Egyptian deities by the Minoans; Egyptian objects discovered in the Aegean and Aegean goods in Egypt; and the depiction of Minoan and Mycenaean tribute bearers in a number of tombs of high ranking eighteenth dynasty officials at Thebes.

Initial assessments of the historical significance of these phenomena were expansive. So, the great Egyptian archaeologist Flinders Petrie created a "Libyo-Greek civilization" out of vague similarities between Egyptian and Mycenaean pottery.[42]

---

thesis. A good example is C. G. Seligman's attempt to explain similarities between Egyptian and Subsaharan African kingship to the purported influence of "an older wide-flung Hamitic stock of which the pre-dynastic Egyptians are the oldest and best known representatives (C. G. Seligman, *Egypt and Negro Africa: A Study in Divine Kingship* [London 1934] 56-58).

[41]The following sections are based on my article "Greek Contact with Egypt and the Levant: Ca. 1600-500 BC. An Overview," *The Ancient World* 27 (1996) 20-28. A useful collection of articles on this theme is John F. Coleman and Clark A. Walz, eds., *Greeks and Barbarians: Essays on the Interactions between Greeks and Non-Greeks in Antiquity and the Consequences of Eurocentrism* (Bethesda 1997).

[42]W. M. Flinders Petrie, "The Egyptian Bases of Greek History," *JHS* 11 (1890) 271-277. For the contemporary debate over Petrie's ideas see

Similarly, the American Egyptologist James Henry Breasted conjured up the "vision of a vanished [sc. Egyptian] empire" that extended from Iraq to Crete on the basis of two Egyptian objects, one found at Cnossus on the island of Crete and the other purchased from an antiquities dealer in Baghdad.[43] Sir Arthur Evans went even further. In *The Palace of Minos* he maintained that his excavations at Cnossus indicated that "Egyptian influences, hitherto reckoned as rather a secondary incident among late classical experiences, are now seen to lie about the very cradle of our civilization."[44]

Such views were widely publicized and even found their way into popular school textbooks. It is not surprising, therefore, that early twentieth century forerunners of contemporary Afrocentrism welcomed the support such interpretations gave to their theories. Thus, in a 1917 article entitled "The African Origin of the Grecian Civilization" George Wells Parker argued that Evans' spectacular discoveries at Cnossus proved that "the ferment creating the wonderful Grecian civilization was preeminently the ferment of African blood."[45] It is equally unsurprising that some later historians, reacting against such exaggerated assessments of Egypt's role in the Aegean, erred in the opposite direction. While evincing a proper skepticism toward some of the more fanciful theories of their predecessors, the general tendency of their criticism was to isolate the Aegean from the eastern Mediterranean as a whole, suggesting that relations between Greece and Egypt in the second millennium BC amounted, in the words of one scholar, to little more than a limited trade in luxuries that floated like a "froth"[46] on the surface of Greek history.

Memphis and Mycenae with supplementary material on the great Chronology debate, David Rohl and Martin Durkin, eds., Isis Occasional Papers, No. 1 (Whitstable, Kent 1988).

[43]James Henry Breasted, *A History of Egypt* (New York 1905; rpt. 1964) 182.

[44]Sir Arthur Evans, *The Palace of Minos: A Comparative Account of the Successive Stages of the Early Cretan Civilization as Illustrated by the Discoveries at Knossos,* 5 vols. (London 1921-1935) 1, 19.

[45]George Wells Parker, "The African Origin of the Grecian Civilization," *The Journal of Negro History* 2 (1917) 343.

[46]The phrase is that of Emily Vermeule, *Greece in the Bronze Age* (Chicago 1964) 151.

The passage of time and new evidence have made clear, however, that, while there can be no question of an Egyptian empire in the Aegean, ties between Egypt and Greece were far more extensive and important in the mid-second millennium BC than a mere "froth". The evidence supporting these new interpretations is varied and includes: Egyptian scenes in Late Minoan I frescoes from Thera, frescoes executed in a Minoanizing style at the Hyksos capital of Avaris in an early eighteenth dynasty context, the Aegean itinerary inscription from the mortuary temple of Amenhotep III at Kom el-Hetan, faience objects with the cartouches of Amenhotep II, Amenhotep III and the latter's chief wife Tiy from Mycenae and Tiryns, an illustrated papyrus from Amarna that has been interpreted as containing representations of Aegean soldiers in Egyptian contexts, and the Ulu Burun shipwreck, which is thought to have been bound for the Aegean when it sank, and contained in its extraordinary cargo of Egyptian and Nubian goods a remarkable gold scarab of the famous Egyptian queen Nefertiti.

Disparate though they are, the items in the above list share two characteristics with the tribute bearer reliefs and the Egyptian objects previously discovered in the Aegean: they mostly involve high status luxury goods and they were found predominantly in governmental centers. In other words, relations between the Aegean and Egypt in the mid-second millennium BC were relatively close, but they were primarily at the state level and involved relatively few people. As a result, when Mycenaean civilization collapsed at the end of the second millennium BC, direct contact between Greece and Egypt ceased, leaving little evidence of long term impact on the development of Greek culture.

The situation is different with regard to the second period of intensive Greek contact with Egypt, that which began in the first half of the seventh century BC and ended in the late sixth century BC with the Persian conquest of Egypt. Our general understanding of the history of relations between Greece and Egypt in this period has not changed materially, and that was to be expected. The principal features of that history—the decisive contribution made by Greek and Carian mercenaries to the liberation of Egypt from Assyrian rule in the 650s BC, the establishment of a Greek diaspora in Egypt in the seventh and sixth centuries BC, the important role played by the city of Naucratis as the center of Greek life in Egypt, and the development of a virtual Egyptomania in late Archaic

Greece—were all well known from Greek literature. Nevertheless, while the main outlines of the story have remained largely unchanged, it has received some unexpected nuances.

Until recently, historians have assumed that the Greeks who settled in Egypt during this period lived in virtual ghettoes with little contact with Egyptian society or culture. One scholar even asserted that "we have no Egyptian evidence that a pre-Ptolemaic priest of any description ever met a Greek,"[47] despite the fact the Greek mercenaries in Saite Egypt served under the command of Egyptian officers who were also priests. Two recently published documents suggest a very different picture of the possibilities open to ambitious Greeks in seventh and sixth century BC Egypt. The first is a Demotic papyrus from Hermopolis dated to the year 575 BC[48] and containing a petition from a priest of Thoth to an Egyptian district official named Ariston, that is, a Greek in Egyptian service, requesting that the latter assist a group of priests who were bringing a dead sacred Ibis to the Fayum for burial. The second is an Egyptian block statue discovered at Priene in western Turkey and published by Olivier Masson and Jean Yoyotte, and containing the following inscription:[49]

> Pedon, the son of Amphinoos, dedicated me, having brought me from Egypt. The Egyptian king Psammetichus gave him a gold arm-band as a reward for bravery and a city because of his excellence.

Ariston and Pedon clearly were not marginalized individuals but government officials, who were fully integrated into Egyptian society and culture. Moreover, Ariston, at least, was presumably literate in Egyptian while Pedon was sufficiently Egyptianized to choose for his monument in his home town a block statue, the sculptural form traditionally used in Egypt to commemorate the achievements of a successful government official. Likewise, the many fine Egyptian objects discovered in the precinct of Hera on Samos and other Greek sanctuaries strongly suggest that Pedon was not an isolated figure but typical of many east Greeks who

---

[47]O. K. Armayor, "Did Herodotus Ever Go to Egypt?" *Journal of the American Research Center in Egypt* 15 (1978) 65.

[48]El Hussein Omar M. Zaghloul, *Frühdemotische Urkunden aus Hermupolis, Bulletin of the Center of Papyrological Studies* 2 (Cairo, 1985) 23-31.

[49]Olivier Masson and Jean Yoyotte, "Une Inscription ionienne mentionnant Psammétique Ier," *Epigraphica Anatolica* 11 (1988) 171-179.

made their fortunes in Egypt and then returned home "to retire". Moreover, the appropriateness to the honored deities of many of the dedicated Egyptian objects and the soundness of the identifications of Greek and Egyptian gods in classical literature indicate that Greeks, who had lived in Egypt, returned to Greece with more than a superficial understanding of Egyptian religion and culture. The full implications of these and other recent discoveries for our understanding of the significance of Egypt for the development of Greek civilization in the archaic and classical periods are still unclear, but it is likely that it will ultimately be found to extend beyond the arts and religion to include, for example, important aspects of early Greek medicine.[50]

Least clearly understood is the nature and extent of Greek interaction with Egyptian culture during the third period of close relations between Greece and Egypt, the Hellenistic Period. Politically the Hellenistic Period is usually defined as beginning with the occupation of Egypt by Alexander the Great in 332 BC and ending with the death of Cleopatra VII in 30 BC. In terms of culture, however, a more useful definition is one that extends the Hellenistic Period to the end of antiquity.[51] In an Egypt, that was ruled first by Macedonians and then by Rome, Greeks for the first time not only came to constitute a substantial minority of the population of Egypt but they also emerged as its social and cultural elite. Greek became the language of government and culture, and Alexandria, the political, economic, and cultural capital of the country. These facts are well known, but evaluation of their implications for cultural relations between Egyptians and Greeks has been surprisingly negative. Indeed, in recent scholarship the dominant view has been that Greek and Egyptian societies coexisted with little interaction between them.[52]

---

[50]The most recent general survey of Egyptian influence on various aspects of Greek culture including medicine is Erik Iversen, "Egypt in Classical Antiquity: A Résumé," *Hommages à Jean Leclant,* edited by Catherine Berger et al., *Bibliotheque d'Étude* 106, 3 (Cairo 1994) 295-305.

[51]The classic statement of this position in English is Norman H. Baynes, "The Hellenistic Civilization and East Rome," *Byzantine Studies and Other Essays* (London 1955) 1-23.

[52]Cf. Stanley M. Burstein, "The Hellenistic Age," *Ancient History: Recent Work and New Directions,* Stanley M. Burstein et. al. (Claremont 1997) 50-52, for a brief overview of this debate.

Although Egyptians of necessity learned Greek and a few Greek-educated Egyptians, such as the priest and historian Manetho, attempted to correct erroneous views of Egyptian history and culture, Greeks, it is maintained, ignored their works and refused to learn Egyptian, so that, despite a massive expansion of writing on Egypt, Greek awareness and understanding of Egyptian thought remained superficial. As for Egyptian influence on Hellenistic Greek culture, it was supposedly limited to the borrowing of technical aspects of Egyptian culture such as new drugs, the use of the pulse in diagnosis,[53] and the solar calendar;[54] and the creation of artistic fads and artificial cults and deities such as Sarapis. While the view of a segregated Egypt was an understandable reaction against earlier unrealistic interpretations of Hellenistic Egypt as an open society in which a mixed culture composed of the best of Greek and Egyptian civilizations developed, a steadily increasing body of evidence suggests that the view of Greek and Egyptian societies existing as hermetically sealed entities within Graeco-Roman Egypt also oversimplifies a complex reality.

Far from being hermetically sealed, Greek and Egyptian societies actually became more and more permeable during the Hellenistic Period. Intermarriage was not uncommon, and Greek identity could increasingly be acquired through education and wealth, especially after Caracalla's extension of Roman citizenship to almost all inhabitants of the Roman Empire in 212 AD erased the sharp distinction between Greeks and barbarians within the Mediterranean basin that had been central to Greek thought since the fifth century BC. The result was the emergence of a growing class of bilingual and bicultural Egyptians, who integrated Greek ideas and Egyptian tradition in a new form of Egyptian thought that was accessible to Greek thinkers and formed an important part of the cosmopolitan form of Greek culture historians call "Hellenism", that was central to both pagan and Christian thought in late antiquity.[55]

The influence of these Hellenized Egyptians is readily apparent in many areas of late ancient thought: in sciences and pseudo-sciences such as astronomy and astrology, magic and

---

[53]Robert K. Ritner, "Innovations and Adaptations in Ancient Egyptian Medicine," *Journal of Near Eastern Studies* 59 (2000) 107-117.

[54]E. J. Bickerman, *Chronology of the Ancient World* (Ithaca 1968) 38-43.

[55]G. W. Bowersock, *Hellenism in Late Antiquity* (Ann Arbor 1990).

alchemy;[56] in religion in the transformation of Egyptian deities such as Isis into universal and potent forces that early Christians saw as formidable threats to their new revelation;[57] and, of course, in philosophy in the development of the mystical theology known as Hemeticism that exercised a powerful influence on such important early modern thinkers as Pico della Mirandola and Giordano Bruno in Italy and Isaac Newton in England.[58] Perhaps, the most remarkable and long-lasting of all of their achievements, however, was the creation of the image of Egypt as the home of primordial wisdom created and preserved by philosopher priests that is at the heart of Bernal's "Ancient Model" with which this paper began and which dominated Egyptian historiography until Champollion's decipherment of hieroglyphics in the early nineteenth century provided the key to the Egyptian past.[59]

This paper has of necessity ranged widely. Afrocentric history is not a passing fad but heir to a long tradition of African American interest in ancient history. Studying it opens the door to a little known but significant aspect of the history of the classics in the United States, and their role in Black education and culture.[60] The questions it raises concerning the significance of Egyptian and Egyptian culture in the formation and development of ancient Greek civilization are also important, but the tools of Afrocentric history are too blunt to provide satisfactory answers.

---

[56]Cf. most recently David Frankfurter, "The Magic of Writing and the Writing of Magic: The Power of the Word in Egyptian and Greek Traditions," *Helios* 21 (1994) 189-221.

[57]The fullest recent treatment of late Egyptian religion is David Frankfurter, *Religion in Roman Egypt: Assimilation and Resistance* (Princeton 1998).

[58]The Egyptian origin of Hermeticism is now generally admitted; cf. especially E. Iversen, *Egyptian and Hermetic Doctrine* (Copenhagen 1984) and Garth Fowden, *The Egyptian Hermes: A Historical Approach to the Late Pagan Mind* (Cambridge 1986).

[59]Cf. Stanley M. Burstein, "Images of Egypt in Greek Historiography," *Ancient Egyptian Literature: History & Forms*, ed. Antonio Loprieno (Leiden 1996) 590-604.

[60]Cf. Shelley P. Haley, "Classics pedagogy begs race questions," *The American Classical League Newsletter* 16,1 (1993) 8-14; and Michele Valerie Ronnick, "Three Nineteenth-Century Classicists of African Descent, *Scholia: Natal Studies in Classical Antiquity* 6 (1977) 11-18.

In studies of the relationships between cultures, it is not enough simply to catalogue borrowed traits and their source; one must also explain if possible why those traits were borrowed and how they were transformed to fit the needs of their new cultural setting. In concrete terms, the Egyptian roots of Greek sculpture and the Phoenician origin of the Greek alphabet are generally recognized, but the early Greek male statue type known as a *Kouros* is not an Egyptian statue type despite its obvious Egyptian ancestry and the function of literacy in Greek society and culture differs significantly from that of alphabet's homeland. Explaining the reasons for those differences is fully as important to understanding the origins of Greek civilization as identifying their sources, and that is a task that has hardly begun.

II

GENDER STUDIES AND HISTORY:
PARTICIPATION & POWER

Nancy Demand

The origin of Gender Studies lies in contemporary women's history, and thus it is relevant to consider the way in which women's roles have been culturally constructed in the history of the 20th century. The first, really heroic, wave of feminism centered on the issue of the vote. During the Second World War, women were "liberated" in massive numbers to work in the wartime economy. Peace then sent them back to the kitchen and family affairs when jobs were needed for returning veterans. The wave of feminism arose again in the 1960s as "liberation" again became a popular concept with the Civil Rights Movement and the opposition to the Vietnam War, a theme picked up by women (partly as a result of the subordinate status many radical groups allotted to women in their ranks).

The second wave of the feminist movement that began in the '60s has all but disappeared today, as "feminist" has become a term of reproach for many young women. Women's Studies programs have been transmogrified into Gender Studies programs, and Male Studies have become the latest "in" field. As an unrepentant feminist, I find some of this both maddening and amusing. I—and many of my colleagues, especially those of us who chose to marry and have children—quite frankly owe our positions as historians to the opportunities opened up to us through Affirmative Action, and, despite what more recent female PhDs may think, much the same is true of them. Why don't most Chairs today dare to say, "No, I won't hire you because you are a women, a married women, you have children." Why do we have blind submissions for most journals, giving women an equal chance for publication beside their male colleagues?

Just as our lives would have been much different without the Women's Movement, so too would the field of Ancient History have been much different were it not for the changes wrought by the shifting movement that started with "Women's Liberation," and became, today, Gender Studies. Whole new areas of cultural history have been opened up to study, and women of ability share to a much greater extent in academic appointments (especially at the junior level), meeting attendance, and publication. But these are generalities—I am not here engaged with the collecting of statistics (the Women's Classical Caucus is doing admirable work with that), but with scholarly work and publications in Ancient History as these have been affected by this train of events, which I shall sum up simply as "Gender Studies."

Given the popularity during the last decade of the various aspects of Gender Studies, and the vast bibliography engendered by this enthusiasm, assessing its effects on work in Ancient History is a formidable assignment. Limitations are imperative. Factors of personal orientation inevitably provide some of these limitations. As a historian, I am most familiar with work in Greek history, and, although I have sought to extend my view beyond this, I am sure that experts in Greek and Roman history could add much that has escaped my attention. On the one hand, my own personal viewpoint is reflected in the inclusion of work in the history of medicine that deals with women. I have not, on the other hand, included material specifically about women in religion, aside from the areas of medicine and magic. Limitations of space, and utility for an undergraduate as well as a graduate audience, have suggested limiting the review to English language publications. (This is at least in part justified by the fact that much of the work in Gender studies is currently being done in English and French, with important works in French usually available in translation.)

The primary focus of this paper is indicated in the subtitle: participation and power. My emphasis is on recent work that refines the picture of participation and power, especially outside the home, by women of all classes.[1] I focus on studies involving women, rather than gay men, because the ground-breaking work ground-breaking work on male homosexuality appeared in 1990

---

[1]Despite the doubts of Barbara McManus, *Classics and Feminism: Rendering the Classics* (New York 1997) 7, that Women's Studies has contributed significantly to political history.

or before.[2] Similarly, the major work on symposia as scenes of men's political activity appeared in 1990.[3] As for lesbianism, I have found nothing that really fits my focus on the public arena. And as for the newest "in" Gender topic, Masculinities, I bypass this as well, for reasons that I shall defend at the end of this paper.

It is indisputable that women were not official participants in political life in any of the states of the classical world. Even so, many degrees of political and social participation involving less than that of full citizenship were possible, and indeed were found in different ancient societies. These range from total seclusion in the house and behind the veil to freedom to move about the city, engage in business, own property, but not to engage formally in political activities. Often the exclusions were very subtle, but their variations obviously would have made a great deal of difference in the lives of women. Current work focuses more and more on refining the picture given by the sources, being especially sensitive to cultural factors that may have shaped the ancient evidence.

I begin with a question that attracted scholars well before the most recent wave of feminism—the status of women in classical Athens. The topic continues to draw much interest, especially in terms of the effect of democracy on women's position. At one extreme we have what has been called the Realist position, as represented by Sue Blundell, which holds that "the development of democracy...[was] a parallel phenomenon to the subordination of women."[4] Similarly, Ian Morris sees the eighth century as the point at which the divide between inner/female and outer/male spheres in the city began to be embodied in the domestic architecture of the courtyard house. He interprets this as an essential part of the development of a "middling" political norm that became "democracy":[5]

---

[2]Sir Kenneth J. Dover, *Greek Homosexuality* (Cambridge, MA 1978); D.M. Halperin, *One Hundred Years of Homosexuality* (New York 1990); D.M. Halperin, J.J. Winkler, and F.I. Zeitlin, eds., *Before Sexuality: The Construction of Erotic Experience in the Ancient Greek World* (Princeton 1990); J. J. Winkler, *The Constraints of Desire* (New York 1990).

[3]Oswyn Murray. *Sympotica. A Symposium on the "Symposion"* (Oxford 1990).

[4]Sue Blundell, *Women in Ancient Greece* (Cambridge, MA 1994) 5 and 129.

[5]Ian Morris, *Archaeology as Cultural History* (Malden, MA and Oxford 2000) 280-286.

The new identity of the male citizen was created, and along with it the preconditions for extreme gender inequality, large-scale chattel slavery, male democracy, and an astonishing cultural explosion. A mixed bag indeed.[6]

At the other end of this ideological divide, scholars look at women's lives in order to find hidden sources of power. The argument here is that if women had such powers there would be less weight to the suggestion that democracy was problematical for women.

One basic problem with such an analysis of power is that it views women's lives through the lens of the current antifeminist backlash, rather than of ancient Greek society itself. For the Greco-Romans, the use of female wiles, seduction, indirection and misdirection was a characteristic, not of a person of power, but of "the intellectually and socially disenfranchised," of slaves and women:[7]

> Women's and slaves' acts of persuasive speech, devoid of legitimacy in the dominant political order, undergo a process of vilification in all kinds of Greek and Roman literary genres, which exaggerate and demonize their ability to persuade their manly masters.

Nor should we forget that it was not only insanity but also the influence of a woman that rendered an Athenian male citizen's legal acts null and void.[8]

The rejection of feminism that lies at the base of such arguments is revealed in Cheryl Ann Cox's disparagement of Pomeroy's view (in *Goddesses, Whores, Wives, and Slaves*) that women were oppressed by the social system, as "shaped by the anger of the rebirth of the women's movement in the 1970's"—although she does allow Pomeroy some credit for her "recent shift away from legal strictures on women."[9] Nonetheless, Cox criticizes Pomeroy's recent jointly-authored

---

[6]Ian Morris (n.5) 33.

[7]Joy Connolly, "Mastering Corruption: Constructions of Identity in Roman Oratory," in Sheila Murnaghan and Sandra Joshel, *Women and Slaves in Greco-Roman Culture* (London 1998) 130-151, 131-32.

[8]Is. 2.1.20, 26; 6.21; Dem. 46.14,16; 48.54-56.

[9]Cheryl Ann Cox, *Household Interests: Property, Marriage Strategies, and Family Dynamics in Ancient Athens* (Princeton 1998) xvi, n.11. Sarah Pomeroy, *Goddesses, Whores, Wives, and Slaves* (New York 1975).

book, *Women in the Classical World*, as well as Blundell's *Women in Ancient Greece* for following the paradigm.[10]

The rosiest picture of Athenian women's position is provided by Cynthia Patterson, in *The Family in Greek History*[11] who argues that democracy opened up a new world for Athenian women's history. She claims to be the first to correct the "19th century paradigm" of women's peculiar repression in democratic Athens,[12] and to refute the "general principle of an inverse relation between the development of Athenian democracy and the status of Athenian women...."[13] In fact, Patterson argues that Athenian women were better off under the democracy by virtue of their secure and protected position within the *oikos*. Again, the feminist backlash seems to be a paramount factor in the interpretation of the evidence.

Lin Foxhall carries a similar argument to much different conclusions.[14] She also sees women as a vital element in Athenian households, and, since households "reproduced the political institutions of a city,"[15] argues that women "penetrated even apparently exclusively male 'public' arenas" (she focuses here on fountain houses). Nevertheless, she cites Greek literary sources that portray male fantasies of women conspiring against men: "women are perceived and portrayed as acting against the autonomy and the interests of an individual man (or men) via

---

[10]E. Fantham, H. Foley, N. Kampen, S. Pomeroy, and H.A. Shapiro, *Women in the Classical World* (Oxford 1994).

[11]Cynthia Patterson, *The Family in Greek History* (Cambridge MA 1998).

[12]Patterson (n.11) 7. Patterson indicts almost every previous scholar in the field, noting only a few exceptions to the acceptance of this paradigm: Josine Blok, "Sexual Asymmetry: A Historiographical Essay," in *Sexual Asymmetry*, ed., J. Blok and P. Mason (Amsterdam 1987) 1-57; Beate Wagner-Hasel, "Das Privat wird politisch," in *Weiblichkeit in geschichtlecher Perspektive*, ed. A.J.Becher and J.Rusen (Frankfurt 1988); idem, "Frauenleben in orientalischer Abgeschlossenheit?" *Der Altsprachliche Unterricht* 2 (1989) 18-29; Marilyn Katz, "Ideology and "the Status of Women' in Ancient Greece," *History and Theory* 31 (1992) 70-97.

[13]Patterson (n.11) 129.

[14]Lin Foxhall, "Pandora Unbound: A Feminist Critique of Foucault's *History of Sexuality*," in D.H.J. Larmour, P.A. Miller, and C. Platter, *Rethinking Sexuality: Foucault and Classical Antiquity* (Princeton 1997) 122-37.

[15]Foxhall (n.14) 129.

[kinship] relationships and bonds over which the man is not fully in control."[16] Nor is her conclusion entirely optimistic. I would not argue that women in classical Greece were not oppressed, but I would maintain that they resisted suppression. The dominant masculinist ideologies which ruled political life and serve as the context for the creation of most of the "surviving source material never completely drowned out the other voices in the Greek conversations we can still hear."[17]

Another somewhat similar view of women's role in the *oikos* is revealed by Steven Johnstone's use of new methodologies of dispute theory and "reading silence" to analyze the evidence for the effects of democracy on women's lives.[18] He argues that "the *oikos* was an ideological construct which, far from representing the 'sphere' of women, was employed in legal narratives to attribute to women subject positions which reinforced male dominance."[19]

Taking a "middling" position on the issue, and opening the way for continued work, Kurt Raaflaub in the AHA's fifth monograph, *Ancient History: Recent Work and New Directions*, finds that our understanding of the question of the effect of democracy on women's situation is still somewhat unsatisfactory.[20] Thus the uneasy question still lurks—did (Athenian) democracy itself make women's lives more narrow and confined? The study of ancient medicine provides unusual insights into the ordinary lives of women in ancient Greece and into the issue of female control. Until the women's movement, scholars studying the Hippocratic Corpus deemed the gynaecological treatises to be unworthy of attention, although the major works make up about an eighth of the entire collection, with the minor works added to this.[21] These texts were simply left

---

[16]Foxhall (n.14) 131.

[17]Foxhall (n.14) 137.

[18]Steven Johnson, "Cracking the code of silence: Athenian legal oratory and the histories of slaves and women," in S. Murnaghan and S. Joshel, *Women & Slaves in Greco-Roman Culture* (London 1998) 221-235.

[19]Johnson (n.18) 229.

[20]Kurt Raaflaub, "Greece," in Stanley M.Burstein, Ramsay MacMullen, Kurt A. Raaflaub, and Allen M. Ward, directed by Carol G. Thomas, *Ancient History: Recent Work and New Directions* (Claremont CA 1997) 26-27, nn. 94-96.

[21]Hermann Grensemann, *Knidische Medizin*. Teil II, *Versuch einer weiteren Analyse der Schicht A in den pseudohippokratischen Schriften de*

unedited and untranslated (with the exception of the great Littré edition, with French translation, in 1839). Other aspects of medical care usually associated with women were also neglected, in particular, the question of whether they sought to control their reproductivity, as well as their possible roles in the transmission of drug lore and magical practices.

Recent work on the gynaeological treatises by Ann Hanson,[22] Lesley Dean Jones[23] and Helen King[24] and on the cultural context of Greek medical practices,[25] has opened up new perspectives on women in the history of medicine, however. The possibility that women sought to control their reproductivity is suggested by passages in the Hippocratic treatises in which doctors claim that abortion is something women are "always doing" (*Diseases of Women* 1.67), express uncertainty about whether a woman who had aborted "may have taken something," (*Epid* V.53), and the statement that "experienced" women knew how to avoids pregnancy (*Nat.Child* 13; *Genit.* 5). This hypothesis of female control is also supported by the presence of many recipes in the gynaecological treatises for "bringing down the menses," hastening labor, or preventing pregnancy. That many plants used in Greek medicine had abortifacient and perhaps contraceptive properties is shown by John Riddle's

---

natura muliebri und de miliebribus I und II. Hermes Einzelschriften (Wiesbaden 1987) 11.

[22]Ann Hanson, "Hippocrates: Diseases of Women I," *Signs* 1 (1975) 567-84; "The Eighth Month Child: Obsit Omen," *Bulletin of the History of Medicine* 61 (1987) 589-602.

[23]Lesley Dean Jones, *Women's Bodies in Classical Greek Science* (Oxford 1992); "Medicine: The 'Proof' of Anatomy," in Fantham *et al.* (n.10) 183-205.

[24]Helen King, *Hippocrates' Woman: Reading the Female Body in Ancient Greece* (London 1998), which includes updates of articles published elsewhere and some new essays.

[25]Ph.J. van der Eijk, H.F.J. Horstmanshoff, P.H. Schrijvers, *Ancient Medicine in its Socio-Cultural Context: Papers Read at the Conress Held at Leiden University 13-15 April, 1992*, 2 vols. (Amsterdam 1995); Heinrich Von Staden, "Women, Dirt and Exotica in the Hippocratic Corpus," *Helios* 19 (1992) 7-30; Nancy Demand, *Birth, Death and Motherhood in Classical Greece* (Baltimore 1994)

studies on plant and drugs.[26] Riddle supports the suggestion by Alline Rouselle that these recipes were women's lore by pointing out evidence for the apparent unfamiliarity with the material on the part of the (male) transcribers of this information, suggesting that they may not have been the original source of the material.[27] Thus primary (if unsanctioned) control of reproductivity may have lain in the hands of women (however, men's suspicions may have magnified the degree of female control).

Turning to another aspect of women and drugs, much of the evidence purporting to associate women especially with the use of drugs as aphrodisiacs and (accidentally or on purpose) poisons (as in Antiphon's speech, *Against the Stepmother*), may have been tainted by invective. This can be seen in the comparison between literature, where the lovesick person is usually female, and the *Papyri Graecae Magicae*, where the seducer is usually male.[28]

Moving to the question of the role that individual elite women may have played in Classical Athens, we find a good example of the effect of rhetoric on our evidence in the material on Aspasia, the "companion" of Pericles, as this has been analyzed by Madeline Henry in her recent book, *Prisoner of History: Aspasia of Miletus and her Biographical Tradition*.[29] Aspasia is known from contemporary ancient sources as the mistress of Pericles, and as a *hetaira* (high-class call girl) and madam. Comic poets claimed that Pericles started the Peloponnesian War at her behest. The Platonic dialogue *Menexenus* claimed that she was the author of a state funeral oration (like Pericles). She was also said to have been a teacher of Socrates. Henry, however, has convincingly demonstrated that these sources present us not with the 'real Aspasia', but with a literary type-figure seen through the eyes of male authors, who used it to transmit gendered cultural messages

---

[26]John Riddle, *Contraception and Abortion from the Ancient World to the Renaissance* (Cambridge, MA 1992); *Eve's Herbs: A History of Contraception and Abortion in the West* (Cambridge, MA 1997).

[27]Aline Rousselle, "Observation feminine et idéogie masculine: le corps de la femme d'après les médicins grecs." *Annales (ESC)* 35 (1980) 1089-115; on the dispute, see Demand (n.25) 63-65.

[28]John Winkler, "The Constraints of Eros," in Christopher A. Faraone and Dirk Obbink, (eds.) *Magika Hiera: Ancient Greek Magic and Religion* (Oxford 1991) 214-243, 224-27.

[29]Madeline Henry, *Prisoner of History: Aspasia of Miletus and her Biographical Tradition* (Oxford 1995).

to their male audience. In fact, all that can reliably be known of Aspasia comes from a fourth-century funerary inscription which may have commemorated several of her collateral descendants. If it has been correctly interpreted, Aspasia was a member of an upper-class family in Miletus, related by her sister's marriage to Alcibiades, grandfather of the charismatic Alcibiades, who was raised in the household of Pericles. She was probably brought to Athens by her family during the turbulent political strife in Miletus in the fifth century, and would naturally have become known to Pericles through her connections with the family of Alcibiades. The key-word that applies to her presentation in the ancient sources is *invective*: in good rhetorical fashion, a male authority figure was attacked through criticisms against a woman with whom he was closely (and probably legitimately) associated.[30]

In Hellenistic history, we find more apparently trustworthy evidence for women's roles in public life, much of it in the form of inscriptions honoring women for benefactions. But this material must be read in its cultural context, and examined for clues as to the actual role that was being played by the women involved. For example, Riet Van Bremen's *The Limits of Participation: Women and Civic Life in the Greek East in the Hellenistic and Roman Periods*,[31] analyses the question of participation and power among elite women in the Greek East. During these periods and in these areas, women appear prominently in the epigraphic record as public benefactors, using their private wealth to provide the city with buildings, public festivals and games, and distributions of food, wine, or money. They appear as recipients of crowns, statues, front seats at the theater or games, and, of course, honorific inscriptions. Van Bremen argues convincingly, however, that these women, although acting in public and sometimes fulfilling the same roles as wealthy men, were acting as members of their wealthy families, and not as independent women as we understand the term.

---

[30]Robert B. Kedrick, in his book *Greek People* (Mountain View, CA 1996) Ch. 6, uses Aspasia as a "hook" on which to hang a discussion of Periclean Athens; he takes the biased evidence as factual, providing those who use this otherwise interesting text in their teaching with a good illustration of the need for assessment of gender-biased sources.

[31]Riet Van Bremen's *The Limits of Participation: Women and Civic Life in the Greek East in the Hellenistic and Roman Periods* (Amsterdam 1996).

In contrast, Ramsay MacMullen in discussing the western Empire in the AAH monograph,[32] *Ancient History: Recent Work and New Directions*, offers another view of the epigraphic sources. He cites the Vindolanda tablets, which contain the earliest autograph by a woman, Sulpicia Lepidina;[33] the documents of Babatha in the *Papyrus Yadin*, which include marriage contracts, property transfers, and the account of a protracted lawsuit over the custody of Babatha's son;[34] the Oxyrhynchus papyrus, with evidence for women engaged in economic activities;[35] and the inscriptions from Ostia, also documenting women's economic activities.[36] He contrasts these actively engaged women with the more limited picture of women's power that Van Bremen finds in the Greek east, raising again the question of the nature of women's "power" and emphasizing the need to examine the cultural context before trying to resolve this issue.

Especially valuable work on the issue of women and political power in the Hellenistic world has been done by Elizabeth Carney, who has studied the role played by Macedonian royal women in the workings of the Macedonian monarchy.[37] Carney stresses the informal, and shifting, roles played by these women, whose influence was made possible by their inclusion as essential members of the royal clan. What these women could do depended on their circumstances, and not on any office (similarly, Kings did not occupy an "office" but ruled by virtue of membership in the clan and raw ability to maintain power by military success). Nonetheless, royal women were often able to exercise a "discrete

---

[32]Ramsay MacMullen, "The Roman Empire," in Burstein, MacMullen, Raaflaub, and Ward (n.20) 79-102, 81-82.

[33]S. Treggiari, *Roman Marriage* (Oxford 1991) 422; A.K. Bosman and J.D. Thomas, "New writing-tablets from Vindolanda," *Britannia* 21 (1986) 299ff.

[34]N. Lewis, ed. *The Documents from the Bar Kokhba Period in the Cave of Letters, Greek Papyri* (Jerusalem 1989), summarized in Goodman, "Babatha's story," *JRS* 81 (1991) 169-75.

[35]E. Kutzner, *Untersuchungen zur Stellung der Frau im römischen-oxyrhynchus* (Frankfort: 1989) 39, 82-98, 107.

[36]H.E. Herzig, "Frauen in Ostia. Ein Beitrag zur Sozialgeschichte der Hafenstade," *Historia* 32 (1983) 77-92.

[37]Elizabeth Donnelly Carney, *Women and Monarchy in Macedonia* (Norman OK 1994). Carney has also published a number of articles, to which reference is made in her text, and which are included in her bibliography.

implementation of power" which was publicly denied but "privately tolerate[d] and even encourage[d].[38] Their activities help to define the Macedonian monarchy, and hence contribute to our knowledge of political history. Among the virtues of Carney's book is a section discussing the problems involved in working with the ancient sources on prominent women. These include the dearth of references, the absence of normative material, an Athenocentric focus, the difficulty of interpreting silence, the bias of the ancient sources against women (especially powerful women) expressed in invective, the problems of assessing anecdotal evidence, and the effects of twentieth-century prejudice.[39] This short section should be required reading for all graduate students in ancient history.

Turning to the Roman world, an aspect of elite women's alleged political activity that is known even to undergraduate students of Roman history is the active role attributed to some notorious women associated with the Roman emperors. Agrippina is especially noteworthy here, and A. Barrett's, *Agrippina: Sex, Power, and Politics in the Early Empire*[40] is an attempt, if not entirely convincing, at rehabilitation. Another noted elite Roman victim of the animosity of the sources is Messalina. Sandra Joshel employs the methodology of rhetoric to reveal her role in Tacitus' portrayal as "a sign in Roman imperial discourse"—her decadence and corruption stand in for the emperor's household and for his imperial power.[41] In general, and aside from the invective-laden literary sources, however, Phyllis Culham argues that "Augustan legislation opened new social and economic horizons for elite women."[42]

In dealing with non-elite Romans, Sandra Joshel's *Work, Identity and Legal Status at Rome*[43] provides a very valuable model Her book is noteworthy in using epigraphical evidence to

---

[38]Carney (n.37) 10.

[39]Carney (n.37) 8-13.

[40]A. Barrett, *Agrippina: Sex, Power, and Politics in the Early Empire* (New Haven 1996).

[41]Sandra Joshel, "Desire, Empire, and Tacitus's Messalina," *Signs* 21 (1995) 50-82, quotation from p. 77.

[42]Phyllis Culham, "Did Roman Women have an Empire?" in *Inventing Ancient Culture: Historicism, Periodization, and the Ancient World*, ed. M. Golden, P. Toohey (London 1997) 102-34.

[43]Sandra Joshel, *Work, Identity and Legal Status at Rome* (Norman OK 1992).

reveal attitudes toward work among ordinary women and men (freedmen and slaves). Here we are given an idea of what their activities in the public sphere actually meant to non-elite women in Rome. Joshel reveals that these people took pride in their occupations and sought to memorialize their accomplishments on their grave memorials, much as did the elite.

In conclusion, I believe that recent work on women in ancient history has profited in the last decade by a closer and more sophisticated analysis of the evidence, including an increased awareness of the cultural context in which it was produced. For the evidence about elite women, this context was often that of the rhetorical scene, and the "evidence" has turned out to be more a matter of invective—attacks on the men associated with these women—than a matter of "truth." For the vast majority of women, non-elite women and often anonymous, it seems that the evidence can sometimes be refined by new methodologies to offer a more nuanced picture of the realities of their lives.

Now, what about men, who have recently become "the problem of the day" in Classical Studies.[44] Inevitably, in the course of work on women in antiquity, much has also been learned about men's gender roles, and Women's Studies has been transmuted into Gender Studies. Moreover, sources on men have always been the standard in ancient history, and they have generally been very well exploited (as I noted above on male homosexuality and on the symposium). Thus it seems unlikely that as much innovation will result from turning our attention now to Men and Masculinities as we have gained from the search for evidence revealing the lives of women. As Kirk Ormand has said in his review of Nicole Loraux, *The Experiences of Tiresias: The Feminine and the Greek Man*, "...in important ways, the work of feminist classicists for the last thirty years or so has already, to a large extent, explored the non-

---

[44]One should note that *Nicole Loraux, The Experiences of Tiresias: The Feminine and the Greek Man* (Princeton, 1995), who recycles a number of earlier articles focusing on the idea that the masculine, also encompasses the feminine (although she does not do justice to the Greek disparagement of the feminine when it appeared in the masculine); Lin Foxhall and John Salmon, eds. *Thinking Men: Masculinity and its Self-Representation in the Classical Tradition* (London and New York 1998) and *When Men were Men: Masculinity, Power and Identity in Classical Antiquity* (Leicester 1999).

neutral, politically loaded construct that is manhood in Greece and Rome."[45]

---

[45]Kirk Ormand, Review of Foxhall and Salmon (1998) in *Bryn Mawr Classical Review* 4 (1999), available at
http://ccat.sas.upenn.edu/bmcr/1999/ 999-04-21.html.

III

ARCHAEOLOGY & ANCIENT GREEK HISTORY

Ian Morris

1. INTRODUCTION

Archaeology is to ancient historians what democracy is to politicians: everyone is for it, yet surprisingly few do it. In this essay I ask what role archaeological data should play in the study of Greek history. To do this, I try to answer three questions:

1. What do we, as ancient historians, want archaeology to do for us?

2. Why is it (on the whole) not doing these things?

3. How should we do the archaeological history of Greece?

2. KEY CONCEPTS

Let's begin with some necessary definitions. The recent boom in interest in late antiquity should remind us that the category *ancient* is not fixed in stone; its boundaries are the outcomes of interpretive processes. Similarly, 1990s work on ethnicity has made the category *Greek* seem less natural than it did a few years ago. But my impression is that the majority of people who describe themselves as historians or archaeologists of ancient Greece work on that part of the world where Greek was spoken between about 700 BC and AD 500. Defining the field of study this way involves some high-level theoretical assumptions, not all of which seem very well justified.[1] But for the sake of brevity, I will define both terms pragmatically, and use "ancient Greek" in this sense throughout this essay.

---

[1] I set out my views in "Classical archaeology" in John Bintliff, ed. *The Blackwell Companion to Archaeology* (Oxford forthcoming).

History is more problematic. It has two common uses, to describe past reality and the practice of studying that no-longer-existing reality. Here I concentrate entirely on the second sense. I define history as the study of all past human activities, and past human responses to non-human activities. I do not define it by the kinds of evidence historians use, because doing so would involve pre-judging the answers to the questions listed above.

Finally, *archaeology*. In another context, I took this to mean the study of what survives of the material culture of the people who lived in the past.[2] This broad definition includes manuscripts, inscriptions, and coins, as well as pottery, graves, and chemical residues left in the earth. This makes archaeology and history synonymous. In this essay, I think a narrower definition will be more useful: by archaeology I mean only the study of unwritten (or "mute") artifacts. Coins, papyri, and inscriptions raise acute interpretive problems of their own, but they are of a different order.[3] As with the definition of "ancient Greek," there are boundary disputes that raise important questions, but the written/unwritten dichotomy is probably the most practical place to start a discussion

In the light of these working definitions, I can restate my opening question as follows: what is the best role for artifacts without writing on them in reconstructing the full range of human activities among Greek-speakers between roughly 700 BC and AD 500?

3. WHAT DO WE WANT FROM ARCHAEOLOGY?

We are all familiar with the communicative power of mute artifacts. Clothes, cars, houses, and the rest of our massive system of objects bombard us with signals. It is useful to think about what archaeologists of the future would make of our own societies if confronted solely by its material remains. Setting aside fine but silly works like David Macaulay's *Motel of the Mysteries*,[4] I suspect that they would in fact get a pretty good idea of the state of the world at the start of the third millennium. But whether that is true or not, they would certainly learn more from our artifacts about some of our activities than about others. They could probably write quite a good history of the expansion of

[2]Ian Morris, *Archaeology as Cultural History: Words and Things in Iron Age Greece* (Oxford 2000).

[3]Michael Crawford, ed. *Sources for Ancient History* (Cambridge 1983).

[4]David Macaulay, *The Motel of the Mysteries* (Boston 1979).

technology or the shift in transportation from canals in the eighteenth century to railroads in the nineteenth and interstate highways and airports in the later twentieth (provided that they chose to examine the kind of sites that would provide this information). Archaeologists would have much less access to political narrative, such as foreign policy or the twists and turns of the presidential election of 2000.

These points are obvious, but bear repeating, because—as Anthony Snodgrass pointed out forcefully[5]—ancient historians often forget them. Things are changing, but depressingly often, ancient historians go to the material record to cast light on textual accounts of military and political narratives. Once in a while this pays dividends, as in the exceptional case of excavations in the Teutoburg Forest;[6] but historians who hope to use the ruins of Greek fortresses to cast light on the foreign policies of specific Athenian rhetors are likely to be disappointed.[7] The hard fact is that dating uninscribed artifacts to time-spans anything less than ±25 years usually depends on wishful thinking.[8] Even when we have precisely dated coins or inscriptions, or dendrochronological dates for building timbers, we cannot be sure when the objects in question entered sealed archaeological deposits. There has been some excellent work in the New World on abandonment processes and the formation of the archaeological record,[9] but it does not seem to be much read by Hellenists. We might guess that on the whole, cheap pottery would not stay in use for much more than a generation. If we are writing a long-term economic or social history, that margin of error may not be too much of a problem. But if we want to use archaeology to illuminate the

---

[5]Anthony Snodgrass, *An Archaeology of Greece* (Berkeley 1987).

[6]Wolfgang Schlüter, "The Battle of the Teutoburg Forest: archaeological research at Kalkeise near Osnabrück." in J. D. Creighton and Roger Wilson, eds. *Roman Germany: Studies in Cultural Interaction, Journal of Roman Archaeology,* supp., Vol.32 (1999).

[7]Josiah Ober, *Fortress Attica* (Leiden1985), Mark Munn, *The Defense of Attica* (Berkeley 1993).

[8] Robert M. Cook, "A note on the absolute chronologies of the eighth and seventh centuries B.C.", *Annual of the British School at Athens* (1969) 64: 13-15.

[9]Particularly good are Brian Schiffer, "Is there a Pompeii premise?" *Journal of Anthropological Research* (1985) 41: 18-41. Catherine Cameron and Steve Tomka, eds. *Abandonment of Settlements and Regions: Ethnoarchaeological and Archaeological Approaches* (Cambridge 1993).

campaigns of the Peloponnesian War, we will probably have to make unwarranted leaps of faith. We will always want new accounts of military and political events, but should not expect archaeology to feature much in them.

Who, then, should be turning to archaeology? In section 4, I argue that those interested in questions about Greek culture[10] stand to gain most, most quickly; and in section 5 I suggest that there are also major payoffs for questions about economics and social structure.[11]

These suggestions are hardly new. Two decades ago, Snodgrass argued that

> by enlarging their horizons..., ancient history and classical archaeology have also become much closer. Once historians extend their interests from political and military events to social and economic processes, it is obvious that archaeological evidence can offer them far more; once classical archaeologists turn from the outstanding works of art to the totality of material products, then history (thus widely interpreted) will provide them with a more serviceable framework, not least because Greek art is notoriously deficient in historical reference.[12]

He confidently predicted that in the case of archaic Greece "it will be difficult for a future researcher to embark on an historical subject...without becoming involved in archaeological questions, and vice versa," and emphasized that Greece probably has the richest database of any field of historical archaeology in the world.[13] The potential benefits of an archaeological approach to

---

[10]Raymond Williams, *Keywords* (Oxford 1983). "Culture" brings its own massive definitional baggage with it. Raymond Williams, who may have given more thought to its definition than anyone, called it "one of the two or three most complicated words in the English language," and many anthropologists now refuse to use the word, for example, Arjun Appadurai, *Modernity at Large: Cultural Dimensions of Globalization* (Minneapolis 1996) 11-16. In North America, historians' use of the word owes most to Clifford Geertz's "anthropological" interpretation. Clifford Geertz, *The Interpretation of Cultures* (New York 1973) and *Local Knowledge* (New York 1983). But even that commitment is now fragmenting; Sherry Ortner, ed. *The Fate of "Culture": Geertz and Beyond* (Berkeley 1999).

[11]I present my own views on the possibility and desirability of drawing clear lines between discursive culture and prediscursive economies and society in Morris (n.2) 9-24. See also section 6 below.

[12]Anthony Snodgrass, *Archaic Greece: The Age of Experiment* (London 1980) 13.

[13]Anthony Snodgrass (n. 5) 14-35.

Greek cultural, social, and economic history are obvious and large.

4. WHY ARE WE NOT GETTING WHAT WE WANT?

Yet Snodgrass' prediction has only partly come true. In this section, I ask why, and suggest that the answer lies largely in the inertia of scholarly institutions. In the late nineteenth century, when university disciplines were being formalized, classical archaeologists took on a very particular role within the academy. For almost a hundred years, aesthetes and dilettantes had promoted the study of Greek art as the best hope for regenerating western art. Newly professionalized classical archaeologists combined this argument with scientific methods, claiming that they could study the artistic exemplars of Graeco-Roman cultural excellence with the same rigor that philologists brought to classical literature. Rather than seeing themselves as part of a larger archaeological community, or even as a sub-set of ancient historians, classical archaeologists on the whole accepted a limited but secure place within classical scholarship.[14]

The history of scholarship in classical archaeology is varied and fascinating, but—generalizing wildly from the mass of details—at most institutions, in most countries, for most of the twentieth century, teaching and research have been formalist. There has been some consensus that archaeologists need to know the details of the material record and the skills of excavation and recording. They also need to know the political narrative history and the main features of literary culture, so they can see where the art fits into the larger story. They do not need to use material culture to challenge or enlarge historical understanding of Greece. Perhaps because of this, they developed an extraordinary antipathy toward reflection on theory and methods.[15]

In North America students of Greece and Rome normally work in Classics departments, whether their primary interest is in history, archaeology, or literature. This should make it relatively easy for historians and archaeologists to learn each other's fields

---

[14]See, in various ways, Michael Shanks, *Classical Archeology of Greece: Experiences of the Discipline* (London 1996); Suzanne Marchand, *Down from Olympus* (Princeton 1996); Stephen Dyson, *Ancient Marbles to American Shores* (Philadelphia 1998); and Ian Morris (n. 1).

[15]See in particular the debate between James Whitley, "Beazley as theorist," *Antiquity* 71 (1997) 40-47 and John Oakley, "Why study a Greek vase painter?" *Antiquity* 72 (1998) 209-213.

as their questions converge, but such co-adaptation is still the exception rather than the rule. It is easy to blame this on the lingering weight of the dead hand of the past, but in fact there are good practical reasons for the continuing divide. First, compared with many fields in the humanities, both ancient history and classical archaeology involve high sunk costs. Would-be scholars have to master vast quantities of data and learn skills that are not easily transferable. To learn each other's data and skills would mean either giving up some of the topics normally considered essential within each of the disciplines, extending graduate training to unsupportable lengths, or (the most common response) carrying on as before, but hoping that scholars educated in one part of the discipline will, as their careers progress, retool and learn the skills of another. None of these are very satisfactory options. To make things worse, there are few good introductory books that encourage cross-disciplinary work. Most textbooks in ancient history are relentlessly political in focus, and those in classical archaeology rigidly oriented toward connoisseurship. Dramatically better books are now appearing,[16] but the history-archaeology gap remains large in them. And as both fields have become more theoretically and methodologically sophisticated, their practitioners have devoted more time to comparative reading. This is surely a good thing, but studying eighteenth-century France may have a higher pay-off for historians of democratic Athens than Greek archaeology; and studying Neolithic England may be equally rewarding for Greek archaeologists.

We might conclude from this litany of woes that the prospects for archaeological history are bleak. But we should bear in mind that scholars in every field struggle with similar problems of finding the right balance between ever-increasing amounts of specialized knowledge and the demands of interdisciplinarity. In the 1990s, modern cultural historians managed to break down longstanding history-literature divisions, and scientists have been even more successful in combining biology with physics, chemistry, and technology. Just like them, we will have to pay a price to make archaeological history viable. But also like them, we will probably find that the results more than justify the costs. In the next three sections, I set out my own view of what

---

[16]Sarah Pomeroy, Stanley Burstein, Walter Donlan, and Jennifer Roberts, *Ancient Greece: A Political, Social, and Cultural History* (New York 1999); and James Whitley, *Greek Archaeology* (Cambridge forthcoming).

archaeological history should look like, and in the final section I return to the theme of how we might develop it.

5. CATEGORIES OF ANALYSIS

Snodgrass proposed that the movement of historians toward social and economic questions and of archaeologists toward a wider range of artifacts would inevitably lead to the triumph of archaeological history. But clearly more is required: historians and archaeologists need to adjust their analytical categories to bring texts and artifacts into the same discussions.

Most historians are familiar with Fernand Braudel's division of the flow of time into three levels of events, structures, and geography, the first operating on a day-to-day time scale, the second on a generational scale, and the third moving so slowly that some Annalistes even call it "immobile history."[17] The literature that survives from Athens lends itself well to the history of events from about 510 BC till 307 BC or so, although after that the story is increasingly fragmentary. Texts from or about other cities also work well at the level of events, although not so continuously as at Athens. But very few surviving texts resemble the serial data that Braudel and his successors used for longer-term history. Not surprisingly, few Greek historians have tried to write at the structural or geographical level. Yet this is precisely where archaeological data work best. As noted above, archaeological chronologies can at best work in 25-year phases. At their most refined, the broad patterns that archaeologists document relate to structural time; more often, they connect to processes that operated over centuries, Braudel's geographical time.[18] When Greek historians ask questions about processes

---

[17]Fernand Braudel, *The Mediterranean and the Mediterranean World in the Age of Philip II.* 2 vols. Trs. Siân Reynolds (Glasgow 1972) 21.

[18]I discuss archaeological time in more detail in Ian Morris, "Archaeology and archaic Greek history," in Nick Fisher and Hans van Wees, eds. *Archaic Greece* (London 1998) 68-70; Ian Morris (n.2) 309, 294-306. On the value of Braudel's categories in archaeology, see John Blintiff, *The Annales School and Archaeology* (Leicester 1997); Bernard A. Knapp, ed. *Archaeology, Annales, and Ethnohistory* (Cambridge 1992). And on archaeological time more generally, Geoff Bailey, "Concepts, time-scales and explanation in economic prehistory," in Alison Sheridan and Geoff Bailey, eds. *Economic Archaeology* (Oxford: BAR International Series 96 1981); and "concepts of time in Quaternary prehistory," *Annual Review of Anthropology* 12 (1983) 165-92.

working on structural time, as Stephen Hodkinson does in his excellent study of *Property and Wealth in Classical Sparta*,[19] it makes sense to combine texts and artifacts; it would be very hard to write such a history without doing so. But for historians who are happy with event-history, the literary sources generally suffice within the narrow limits mentioned above; and, conversely, so long as historians limit themselves to the literary sources, they will find have trouble going beyond event-history.

Hodkinson's book illustrates a second point: classical Greek historians who stick with the texts are normally Athenocentric. They have to define problems in Athenian terms, and seek answers in Athenian sources. They can write good histories of what Athenians thought about Sparta, but not such good ones of the Spartans themselves did. There are of course textual sources from outside Athens, particularly from hellenistic times, and good local histories have been written. But on the whole, if we want to examine large-scale geographical processes—precisely those processes that tend to operate at the structural time-level—we are again forced to turn to the archaeological record.

But the analytical categories that dominate classical archaeology are equally ill-suited to archaeological history. Most of the time, classical archaeologists argue about artifacts, whether single art-works or groups of objects of similar type. For the questions that were pressing a hundred years ago, this was a sensible way to proceed. But it works less well if what we want is archaeological history. Instead, we need to focus on *contexts of behavior*—that is, on how objects were used. Archaeology being what it is, we can usually only examine the final stage of the biography of an artifact, at which it entered the archaeological record, whether as a grave good, a votive offering, or garbage left on the floor of a house, thrown into a pit, or dispersed across the landscape with manure. Rather than dividing up objects into fine pottery, coarse pottery, bronze jewelry, statues, etc., as most textbooks and site reports tend to do, we will want to know more about depositional contexts—graves, houses, sanctuaries, refuse dumps, or whatever other activities actually produced the deposits we find. These methods were initially developed by prehistorians working without access to texts, and needing to generate meaning from the material record itself, but they can tell us even more when applied to literate cultures. The contexts of deposition that

---

[19]Stephen Hodkinson, *Property and Wealth in Classical Sparta* (London 2000).

dominate the archaic and classical Greek archaeological record—houses, graves, sanctuaries—are also ones that the Athenian literary sources discuss at length, representing them as major places for the creation and negotiation of meaning.[20]

6. ARCHAEOLOGICAL HISTORY I: IDEOLOGY

Archaeology is all about material culture, and it might seem sensible to assume that if it is relevant to any kind of history, it is going to be a materialist form. In a famous article written almost half a century ago, Christopher Hawkes argued just this, proposing a "ladder of inference." According to Hawkes, archaeological interpretations are most secure when they deal with technology, somewhat less so when they are economic, less secure still in the sphere of social structure, and least secure of all when touching on ideas.[21] But in the last twenty years, archaeologists turned this hierarchy upside-down. Material culture is cultural as well as material, and people use objects to express meanings. Most of the things we recover enter the archaeological record because people chose to put them there, whether through deliberately burying them or casually throwing them away rather than recycling them. Focusing on contexts of deposition foregrounds the fact that archaeologists study not the material world, but the uses that people in the past made of the material world. The archaeological record relates first of all to the symbolic construction of meaning. We learn what people thought it was appropriate to give to the dead and the gods, and what they thought it was appropriate to dispose of in different ways. Once in a while, we can dig up houses destroyed by fire and earthquakes, which come closer to a frozen moment in time; but even in these cases we have to deal with abandonment processes and the post-abandonment recovery of objects. The "Pompeii premise," that the archaeological record simply mirrors the material realities of the past, could not be more wrong.[22]

---

[20]I argue this point in more detail in Ian Morris (n.18) 1-91.

[21]Christopher Hawkes, "Archaeological theory and method: some suggestions from the Old World," *American Anthropologist* 56 (1954) 155-68.

[22]See Lewis Binford, "Behavioral archaeology and the 'Pompeii premise'," *Journal of Anthropological Research* 37 (1981) 195-208; Brian Schiffer (n.9); and for Pompeii itself, Penelope Allison, "Roman households: an

Ian Hodder sums up this issue by suggesting that "in archaeology *all* inference is via material culture. If material culture, all of it, has a symbolic dimension such that the relationship between people and things is affected, then *all* of archaeology, economic and social, is implicated."[23] The literary sources tell us that ancient Greeks, like people in the present, used material culture as a kind of non-verbal language through which they discussed many of the same issues that dominated their verbal conversations. Greek writers represented material culture as something to use creatively, in the same way as words, to construct images of themselves and the world around them. They knew that ways of dressing or building houses were different from speech, but they implicated material culture in the same rhetorical games as words. Material culture was ambiguous, and they felt that it required linguistic interpretation. We make most sense of Greek material culture by using the closest analogies, the Greeks' own discussions of it, and combining words and things into a proper archaeological history of representations.

It would be easy to pile up examples. In our earliest sources, Homer put down much of Odysseus' success to his ability to apply *noesis*, "intelligence," more effectively than anyone else to the material *semata*, or "signs," he came across in his adventures. Throughout the *Odyssey* he identified meanings which eluded others, and took advantage of this to further his own ends. The hero had to be adept at reading non-verbal cues, from architecture to smiles.[24] In later centuries, for which we have more literary evidence, the complexity of reading material culture and its embeddedness in the same contests over meaning as the written sources are very clear. Aeschylus took it for granted that the audience of his *Agamemnon*, staged in 458 BC, would get the nuances of its famous carpet scene. By unrolling a purple carpet between her returning husband's chariot and the entrance to the palace, Clytemnestra trapped Agamemnon between either belittling his own authority by refusing to step on such a symbol of kingliness or hubristically soiling the wealth embodied in the filmy material. The play turned on his vacillation in the face of the

---

archaeological perspective," in Helen Parkins, ed. *Roman Urbanism* (London 1997) 112-46.

[23]Ian Hodder, *Reading the Past*. 2nd ed. (Cambridge:1991).

[24]Gregory Nagy, *Greek Mythology and Poetics* (Ithaca, NY 1990); Donald Lateiner, *Sardonic Smile: Nonverbal Behavior in Homeric Epic* (Ann Arbor 1995).

material trappings of power.[25] Where our evidence is densest, in fourth-century Athens, any good orator knew that a passing reference to hairstyle, choice of cloak, or tableware spoke volumes about his rival's wicked intentions.[26]

Classical historians sometimes respond to the ancient obsession with material culture mechanically. The method is simple: we read the texts, which tell us that object A signifies idea B, etc. Symbolism is a code. We find out what A means, and our job is easy. We look at a carved Roman sarcophagus and can say that the snake means death, the olive means life, the egg is a sign of rebirth, and so on. But while these one-to-one associations are not necessarily wrong, our sources show that things were more complicated. Even when we have texts directly relating to the objects we have dug up, we can rarely assign "the meaning" to an artifact, or assume that it had any such meaning independent of its context of use. A gold cup in a grave meant something very different from one given to a god, or displayed in a dining room. The best example is the so-called "Orphic" graves of the late fourth and third century BC. The people who cremated a man at Derveni in Macedonia around 350 BC used grave goods much like those in other rich burials, but burned with him a papyrus roll describing an afterlife radically different from the mainstream Hades.[27] Gold cups had different religious meanings for different buriers.

Some associations carry over from one context to another, and in that sense we can speak of an irreducible core of meanings given to gold cups by a particular group at a particular moment; but many important meanings were entirely context-dependent. To pour libations to the gods from gold cups as the Athenian fleet sailed for Sicily in 415 BC was a fine and patriotic thing (Thucydides 6.32), but to say that a man took pride in owning gold cups was to imply that he lacked the qualities of the true citizen (Demosthenes 22.75). To say that your enemy went round positively bragging about his cups was even worse—it evoked images of anti-social hubris (Demosthenes 21.133, 158). When Andocides (4.29) wanted to convince a jury that Alcibiades was beyond the pale of civilized society, he took advantage of these

---

[25]Gregory Crane, "The politics of the carpet scene in the Agamemnon," *Classical Philology* 88 (1993) 117-36.

[26]Josiah Ober, *Mass and Elite in Democratic Athens* (Princeton 1989).

[27]Petros Themlis and Yannis Touratsoglou. *Oi Taphoi tou Derveniou* (Athens 1997).

associations by alleging that Alcibiades tried to create the impression that gold vessels belonging to an Athenian embassy were his own, not only pretending that cups made him a better man, but even lying about owning them.

To bury a gold cup with a dead relative may have been even more hubristic. In the roughly 3000 fifth- and fourth-century BC graves known from Athens, there is not a single example of this,[28] although we know from exports to Thrace that Athenian craftsmen made superb precious tableware. The literary sources do not give us "the meaning" of gold cups, which we can then apply to our finds. But they do give a sense of the semantic range of artifacts, the possibilities available to the people who used them, and the limits of plausible interpretation.

Verbal and non-verbal languages are not the same. Clifford Geertz, one of the main advocates of what he calls the "life is a text" model in anthropology, notes that its "proponents incline toward the examination of imaginative forms: jokes, proverbs, popular arts," but have been less successful—indeed, have hardly tried their hands—at examining institutions, worship, or war.[29] The gaps between material culture and texts are even more pronounced. Discussing archaeologists' borrowings from linguistic structuralism, Ernest Gellner observed that "the whole point is this:...the entities used in [linguistic] symbolism and communication operate under a rather special economy, without scarcity. Or, better, the other way around: symbolic systems choose as their units, their vehicles of communication, elements whose cost approaches zero."[30] That is patently not true of the material world, whose symbols are very much governed by rules of scarcity. An Athenian could not just decide to flaunt gold cups, as Andocides' story about Alcibiades, true or not, illustrates. First he had to get hold of some.

We need different intellectual tools to analyze pottery and poetry, but we have to analyze both within the same cultural framework. Pots and poems were used by the same people, who—in case we should be foolish enough to doubt it—repeatedly wrote that they used both to construct and contest categories. The outcomes varied from one context to another, but

---

[28]Ian Morris, *Death-Ritual and Social Structure in Classical Antiquity* (Cambridge 1992) 108-127.

[29]Clifford Geertz, *Local Knowledge* (New York 1983) 33.

[30]Ernest Gellner, *Relativism in the Social Sciences* (Cambridge 1985) 150.

there is no reason other than the defense of academic boundaries for us to lump together all material culture, regardless of context of use, as one discourse and to separate all verbal culture as another, so that we can look for "the mismatch between texts and archaeology [which] can articulate important contradictions between operative social contexts."[31] Borrowing another Geertzian phrase, all these categories of evidence are the remains of models *for* reality as well as models *of* reality.[32] Looking for the intersections of arguments based on such different forms of evidence ties our interpretations to themes that would have made sense to the ancients, and thickens our descriptions.

One of the most productive directions in Greek cultural history in the last decade has been toward the "history of ideologies," reading archaic poetry and Athenian oratory and philosophy against the grain, exposing conflicts in values within the communities producing and using these texts.[33] The texts show that material culture was part of these debates, and archaeology can not only contribute to recent discussions of egalitarianism, citizenship, and gender, but can also transform them, by offering a longer-term and geographically broader perspective.[34] The patterns in material display suggest that classical concerns with civic equality go back as far as the eighth century BC, and that the concept of citizen egalitarianism was in fact in retreat in the fourth century. Further, these ideas were not uniquely Athenian. Athens was part of a nestled hierarchy of regions. Some of the economic trends we discern in the Athenian sources were common to the

---

[31]David Small, "An archaeology of democracy?" in Morris and Raaflaub, eds. *Democracy 2500? Questions and Challenges* (Dubuque, IA 1997) 217-27. I challenge this assumption at greater length in Ian Morris, "Archaeology as a kind of anthropology," in Morris, "Archaeology as a kind of anthropology, in Morris and Raaflaub, ibid (1997) 229-39.

[32]Clifford Geertz. (n.10) 93.

[33]Especially Carol Dougherty, *The Poetics of Colonization* (New York 1993); Carol Dougherty and Leslie Kurke, eds. *Cultural Poetics in Archaic Greece* (Cambridge 1993); Leslie Kurke, *The Traffic in Praise: Pindar and the Poetics of Social Economy* (Ithaca, NY 1991); Leslie Kurke, *Coins, Bodies, Games, and Gold: The Politics of Meaning in Archaic Greece* (Princeton 1999), Andrea Nightingale, *Genres in Dialogue: Plato and the Construct of Philosophy* (Cambridge 1995); Josiah Ober (n.26); Josiah Ober, *Political Dissent in Democratic Athens* (Princeton 1998); Sitta von Reden, *Exchange in Ancient Greece* (London 1995).

[34]I argue this particularly in Ian Morris (n.28) (n.18) and (n.2).

entire Mediterranean basin; but cultural responses to them varied through space as well as time. From at least the eleventh century BC, Athens had much in common with a broader central Aegean region. The patterns in the archaeological record are the outcome of countless individual decision about how to build houses, bury the dead, and so on, so it should not surprise us that no two communities were exactly the same. But the major contribution of archaeology is to show that if we want to understand the central concerns of classical Athenians, we must (a) trace them back several centuries, and (b) think on a panhellenic and even pan-Mediterranean scale.

In moving in this direction, archaeological history parallels developments in Greek art history and in the "postprocessual" branch of archaeological theory.[35] Some of the most interesting work in archaeological theory now comes from scholars combining artifacts and texts in societies as diverse as pharaonic Egypt, early modern England, and nineteenth-century America.[36] Greek archaeological history has the potential to have a major impact in this area, as well as contributing to debates going on among art historians, cultural historians, and literary critics.

7. ARCHAEOLOGICAL HISTORY II: SOCIETY AND ECONOMY

The advantage of thinking of archaeological history as part of a larger history of ideologies is that it allows us to take the archaeological data for what they patently are: the material traces of ancient constructions of meaning. Instead of trying to find some way to get round the ritualized actions that created the material record and reach some underlying reality, the historian of ideologies makes ritual and performance the center of attention.

---

[35]Art history: François Lissarrgue, *The Aesthetics of the Greek Banquet.* Trs. by J. Day (Urbana 1990); Robin Osborne, *Archaic and Classical Greek Art* (Oxford 1998); Michael Shanks, *Art and the Early Greek State: An Interpretive Archaeology* (Cambridge 1999); Andrew Stewart, *Art, Desire, and the Body in Ancient Greece* (Cambridge 1997). Postprocessual archaeology: John Barrett, *Fragments from Antiquity: An Archaeology of Social Life in Britain, 2900-1200 BC* (Oxford 1994); Ian Hodder. *Theory and Method in Archaeology* (London 1995); Ian Hodder, *The Archaeological Process* (Oxford 1999); Christopher Tilley, *Metaphor and Material Culture* (Oxford 1999); Michael Pearson and Michael Shanks, *Theater/Archaeology* (London 2001).

[36]Leslie Kurke (n.33).

This has its merits, and has led to significant advances in interpretation. But it also has its price.

In her pathbreaking discussion of metals and coinage in archaic Greek poetry, Leslie Kurke suggests that

> Because coinage is a polyvalent symbol within a complex symbolic system, the struggle I endeavor to reconstruct is a struggle fought *over* and *in* representation. At issue is who controls signification and who has the power to constitute the culture's fundamental hierarchies of value. While these issues have "real life" implications—for example, in the sociological basis of citizenship and relative status of citizens—such a struggle over fundamental hierarchies of value can only be a discursive one, fought out in the codes of our texts, visual images, and signifying practices over the constitution of the cultural imaginary. Thus, it is not as if there is some "reality" we are struggling to get to behind the texts, images, and practices, if we can just break through their screen by patient source criticism and sifting of "facts." In this "contest of paradigms," the discursive structures of our texts (literary and visual) *are* the "facts" at issue.[37]

For the historian of ideologies, what people say about coinage, or how they use valuable objects in funerals, tell us little about the Greeks' ability to appropriate nature or the equity of their distribution of its fruits, but much about the constitution of the cultural imaginary. Kurke does not explicitly deny that we can ground the evidence in external, nondiscursive economic realities, which would let us ask whether the invention of money stimulated economic growth, or meant that ordinary people lived longer and ate better than before, or allowed a small group to concentrate more of the world's goods in their own hands. But she comes close to doing so, neatly encapsulating the challenge that postmodern historiography poses to economic and social history. If the assumptions behind the cultural history of ideologies are defensible, then traditional socioeconomic history rests on foundations of sand. If they are not defensible, then the history of ideologies is impoverished, producing nothing more than bloodless, intellectual games.

This has been the central epistemological debate in historiography for more than ten years, and I have no illusions that I can resolve it here.[38] But ancient historians can no more

---

[37]Leslie Kurke. (n.33) 23.

[38]There are many discussions of postmodernism in history. I have found the following most useful: Joyce Appleby, Lynn Hunt, and Margaret Jacobs, *Telling the Truth About History* (New York 1994); Robert F. Berkhofer,

afford to neglect it than any other historians, and attempts to bring together verbal and non-verbal evidence in fact foreground it. I suggested above that poetry, oratory, graves, and houses were all different performance contexts within which Greeks represented identities. Historians of ideologies stress the concepts of representation and performance, which allow them to bring together these categories of evidence; while social and economic historians, I suggest, must accept the cultural historians' basic points, but should also stress that we are talking about *different* performance contexts.

Summing up the core propositions of the history of ideologies, Roger Chartier claims that "It is clear from the outset that no text, even the most apparently documentary, even the most 'objective' (for example, a statistical table drawn up by a government agency), maintains a transparent relationship with the reality that it apprehends."[39] That is, there are no neutral reflections of unmediated social realities. We cannot move from how our sources present the world to how the world really is; every presentation is a re-presentation. All we can do is play off one (mis)re-presentation against another. But we might respond to this claim with some of the historian's tried and true methods, setting up a hierarchy of sources. Chartier's statistical table may well have contributed to and been constructed within new concepts of state surveillance, requiring that we read it as part of an argument about what the ideal community should be like. But that does not necessarily invalidate readings which move past form to content. There will always be problems in doing this, but they are of well known types, and historians have tools to tackle them. In some cases the discourse of state control will indeed operate in such a way as to rule out attempts to go beyond form; but that must be demonstrated empirically, not assumed. The same is true when we are reading archaic poetry or analyzing graves: we *might* be trapped in competing language games, but we need empirically grounded demonstrations of this, not blanket theoretical statements.

Beyond the Great Story: History as Text and Discourse (Cambridge, MA 1995); Richard J. Evans, *In Defense of History* (New York 1997); Richard Jenkins, ed. *The Postmodern History Reader* (London 1997); C. Behan McCullagh, *The Truth of History* (London 1998).

[39]Roger Chartier, *Cultural History: Between Practices and Representations*. Trs. Lydia Cochrane (Ithaca, NY 1988).

If, when we read texts (including material culture texts) by authors engaged in different language games, we find that they nonetheless represent an external social/economic reality in similar ways, we are on to something. At the very least we are uncovering shared dispositions cutting across lines which in other contexts act as boundaries; and if the contexts are different enough and numerous enough, we may conclude that for all the complexities of the exercise, we have reached a nondiscursive reality.[40] To take just one example from the thousands of historical examples, when Emmanuel Le Roy Ladurie found that all the sources relating to land distribution in Languedoc from 1400 through 1800 pointed to a cyclical pattern of concentration and dispersal, despite the differences in the motives and cultural worlds of their producers, he was surely right to conclude that there was an increase in the number of middle-sized farms at the expense of very small and very big holdings in the fifteenth century, and that many of these middling properties disappeared in the sixteenth and seventeenth centuries, some breaking into several smaller farms, others being absorbed into larger estates.[41]

What this meant (an interpretive question) and why it happened (a causal question) are different matters. But the important point is that there *are* ways to move outside a world of competing representations. We are dealing not with a theoretical problem, of whether such things as economic and social history can possibly exist, but a methodological one, of how to combine categories of evidence in such a way that we can move beyond the fact of their textuality. But Greek economic archaeology faces severe methodological problems which have rarely been confronted.[42]

---

[40]Cf. Alison Wylie, "The interplay of evidential constraints and political interests: recent archaeological research on gender," *American Antiquity* 57 (1992) 15-35; and counterarguments in Michael Fotiadis, "What is archaeology's mitigated objectivism mitigated by?" *American Antiquity* 59 (1994) 545-55, and Michael Fotiadis, "The historicism of postprocessual archaeology and its pleasures," *Aporemata* 5 (2001) 339-64.

[41]Emmanuel Le Roy Ladurie, *The Peasants of Languedoc.* Trs. J. Day (Urbana 1974) 23-29.

[42]I describe the general state of the field in more detail in Ian Morris, "The social and economic archaeology of Greece: an overview," in R. Docter and E. Moorman, *XVth International Congress of Classical Archaeology, Amsterdam, July 12-17, 1998* (Amsterdam 1999) 27-33.

For example, a huge amount has been written on trade, based largely on fragments of Greek pottery found far from where they were manufactured. We can assume that people moved these pots from one place to another, and so their distribution is logically connected to the circulation of material goods. But connected how? All classicists know that many of the most famous Athenian black- and red-figure vases come from Etruscan tombs. Should we conclude that there was a special pottery trade between Athens and Etruria? Not necessarily. Possibly Etruscan funerary rituals had a special role for Athenian painted pottery, leading to a much higher proportion of the Athenian vases that made their way to Etruria ended up in graves than of those Athenian vases that made their way to southern France, or stayed home in Athens. We might conclude that the pots tell us a lot about Etruscan ritual, but that the ritual acts as a barrier which cuts off the excavated record from the material reality of the circulation of goods through trade or other mechanisms. Alternatively, we might argue that the Etruscans worked with what they had got; if more Athenian pots ended up in graves here than anywhere else, that was because the Etruscans had more of these pots than anyone else.

Neither of these extreme claims seems very plausible, but the way to analyze them is through the manipulation of context. That is, if the prominence of Athenian figured pottery in Etruria as compared to Provence or Athens itself is a function of different funerary rites, then we would expect to find a different pattern if we compare the amounts of Athenian figured pottery found in settlements in Etruria, Provence, and Attica. Approaching the question in this way does not require us to assume that settlement evidence is a transparent window onto the realities of the circulation of goods, exposing the ideological nature of death-rituals. What we dig up in a settlement is as much the product of cultural processes as are grave goods: in different societies, there are different patterns of discard, curation, cleaning, and abandonment. As noted above, the "Pompeii premise" is a serious fallacy. But the crucial point, again, is that the formation processes behind the settlement deposits are *different* from those behind the cemeteries. By comparing proportions of finds from different contexts, we can begin to identify the forces controlling depositional practices.

But this only raises new problems, ones created by archaeologists themselves. No two sites are dug or published in exactly the same ways, and hardly any excavators publish their results in such detail that we can quantify the proportions of different kinds of pottery and say exactly where in a settlement different types of pottery were found. But Grazia Semeraro's recent quantitative study of Greek imports in the heel of Italy shows what can be done, and raises two issues. First, just as Michael Dietler found in southern France, cups and kraters dominate the record, suggesting that traders were supplying demands created by specific ritual activities, above all the adoption or adaptation of Greek-style drinking ceremonies.[43] Second, Greek imports form a rather small percentage of the total ceramic assemblage. Accurate quantification is crucial. If we want to understand the production of and trade in pottery, we must know their scale. We need to know both how many pots were found on sites, and also what proportion of the pots originally made or moved these represent.

There have been several attempts to come up with multipliers to answer the second problem. For one category of pots, the prize amphoras given out at the Panathenaic games every four years, we know roughly the total number originally made, and from this can calculate a recovery rate. In a classic paper, Robert Cook argued for a recovery rate of 0.2 percent, and then applied this to Athenian ceramic production generally, arguing that it was basically a household craft, not an "industry" in the sense we normally understand the word. But even with such a well known category as Panathenaic amphoras, problems abound. Using a slightly different sample, T. B. L. Webster calculated a 0.3 percent recovery rate; and Bentz puts it as high as 1 percent. And

---

[43]Grazia Semeraro, *En Neusi* (1997); Michael Dietler, "The cup of Gyptis: rethinking the colonial encounter in Early Iron Age western Europe and the relevance of world-systems models," *Journal of European Archaeology* 3 (1995) 89-111, and "The Iron Age in Mediterranean France: colonial encounters, entanglements, and transformations," *Journal of World Prehistory* 11 (1997) 269-357; cf. Karim Arafat and Catherine Morgan, "Athens, Etruria and the Heuneburg: mutual misconceptions in the study of Greek barbarian relations," in Ian Morris, ed. *Classical Histories and Modern Archaeologies* (Cambridge 1994) 108-134. Robin Osborne, "Pots, trade and the archaic Greek economy," *Antiquity* 70 (1996) 33-39 uses Rosati's much less detailed catalogue of Athenian black figure pottery from around the Mediterranean to argue that the trade in Athenian pottery was directed toward specific markets by 600 BC, but the samples are rather small for such sweeping conclusions. Rosati L. Quartili, and M.P. Germandi, *La ceramica attica nell Mediterraneo: analisis computerizzate delle diffusione. Le fasi initiali 630-560 a. C.* (Bologna 1989).

archaeologists do not agree on how to relate the Panathenaic amphoras to other categories of pots: Webster argued that probably about 1 percent of all the Greek pottery originally made had then been found, while Ingeborg Scheibler estimated 3 percent, and Eisman no less than 10 percent. Vladimir Stissi, on the other hand, concludes that even the 1 percent recovery rate "is far too high, especially for less finely decorated pots."[44]

These basic questions remain unanswered. Given our uncertainty, it is no surprise that wildly different models have been proposed for the economic mechanisms behind the movements of pottery and other goods. Half a century ago, it was common to assume large quantities of goods in movement. Rostovtzeff hypothesized interconnected markets from Persia to Italy in the fourth century BC and later by extrapolating from the evidence then available; and French archaeologists developed visions of large-scale of trade in the late archaic and classical west Mediterranean.[45] In the last twenty years it has become normal to assume small quantities of goods in movement. Snodgrass has suggested that from the Late Bronze Age through archaic times, gift-giving was a more important channel than market exchange, and David Gill has even argued that Greek pots moved around the

---

[44]Robert M. Cook, "Die Bedeutung der bemalten Keramik für den griechischen Handel," *Jahrbuch des deutschen archäologischen Instituts* 74 (1959) 114-23; T.B.L. Webster. *Athenian Culture and Society* (London 1972); M. Bentz, *Panathenäische Preisamphoren. Eine athenische Vasengattung und ihre Funktion vom 6.4. Jh. V. Chr.* (Basel: Antike Kunst Beiheft 18, 1998): 17-18; Ingenorg Scheibler, *Griechische Topferkunst. Herstellung, Handel und Gebrauch der antiken Tongefasse* (Munich, 1983) 9; M. Eisman, "Nikosthenic amphorai: the J. Paul Getty Museum amphora," *Getty Museum Journal* 1 (1974) 52; Vladimir Stissi, "Why do numbers count? A plea for a wider approach to excavation pottery," in Docter and Moorman (n.42) 405; cf. Lisa Hannestad, "Athenian pottery in Etruria c. 550-470BC," *Acta Archaeologica* 59 (1989) 113-30 on Etruria. On the Athenian pottery as a household industry, see Karim Arafat and Catherine Morgan, "Pots and potters in classical Athens and Corinth," *Oxford Journal of Archaeology* 8 (1989) 311-46.

[45]Michael Rostovtzeff, *Social and Economic history of the Hellenistic World* 3 vols (Oxford 1941) 83-95, 104-125; George Vallet, *Rhégion et Zanclè: histoire, commerce et civilization des cités chalcidiennes du détroit de Messène* (Paris 1958); François Villard. *La céramique grecque de Marseille (V e-IVe siècle): essai d'histoire economic* (Paris 1960).

Mediterranean as ballast—saleable in good weather, but dumped overboard in storms.[46]

The shift from maximizing to minimizing models was theory-driven, as Finley's substantivist vision of ancient economics took hold.[47] But I want to stress that in principle we can test these competing visions empirically, given larger-scale archaeological work, more careful recording, more detailed and consistent publication, and the willingness to put forward quantitative models. Robin Osborne's recent speculation that the Greek settlement at Pithekoussai could only have flourished as it did had there been at least fifty ship voyages per year between it and the Aegean, moving around some 3000-4000 tons of goods, is a good example. I suspect that the population of Pithekoussai was only half the size Osborne estimates, correspondingly reducing the level of trade required, but only by risking such explicit quantitative estimates can we hope to advance our analyses.[48]

I have focused on trade because it has received more attention from classical archaeologists than other economic questions. But it is in fact one of the most problematic topics. We can expect more rapid progress in many other areas. Intensive surface surveys are giving us a whole new way to think about demography. Walter Scheidel has quite fairly likened the methods that Greek historians have used to calculate Athenian population from the literary sources to those of Tolkien buffs in working out the numbers of Elves and Orcs in Middle Earth.[49] There are certainly interpretive problems with the survey evidence, but it represents a quantum leap in the quality of our demographic data.[50] The surveys point to at least a tenfold population increase

---

[46]Anthony Snodgrass, "Heavy freight in archaic Greece," in Peter Gamsey, Keith Hopkins, and C.R. Whittaker, eds. *Trade in the Ancient Economy* (Cambridge 1983) 16-26; Anthony Snodgrass (n.5); David Gill, "Positivism, pots and long-distance trade," in Ian Morris (n.43) 99-107.

[47]Moses I. Finley, *The Ancient Economy* 1st ed. (Berkeley 1973).

[48]Robin Osborne (n.43) 41; Ian Morris, "The absolute chronology of the Greek colonies in Sicily," *Acta Archaeologica* 67 (1996) 57 n. 1.

[49]Walter Scheidel, "Progress and problems in Roman demography," in Walter Scheidel, ed. *Debating Roman Demography* 1-81 (Leiden 2001) n. 195.

[50]See Kostas Sbonias, "Introduction to issues in demography and survey," in John Bintliff and Kostas Sbonias, eds. *Reconstructing Past Population Trends in Mediterranean Europe* (Oxford 1999) 1-20; John Bintliff, Phil Howard, and Anthony Snodgrass, "The hidden landscape of prehistoric

across many parts of the Greek world between the ninth century BC and the fourth, followed by a fifty percent decline across the last three centuries BC.[51] We have hardly begun to think about the economic significance of this. What makes it still more remarkable is that the archaeological evidence for the size of houses and the quality of domestic assemblages suggests that standards of living improved substantially between the ninth century BC and the fourth, even as population was expanding.[52] Both substantivist historians and economists tend to assume that sustained economic growth was impossible before the industrial revolution, because agrarian societies were trapped in a Malthusian cycle: any advance in technology or improvement in climate or the terms of trade would be converted into more mouths to feed, until demand outran production and equilibrium was re-established by emigration, a declining birthrate, or mass death. Yet here we have a half-millennium long period of growth. If the typical standard of living was close to mere subsistence around 900 BC, it was perhaps double that by 300 BC. Combined with ten-fold population increase, this would mean that the total economic output of the Greeks was twenty times higher in the age of Alexander than at the start of the Geometric period. This was no Industrial Revolution, but it defies standard descriptions of

---

Greece," *Journal of Mediterranean Archaeology* 12 (1999) 139-68. Scheidel (n49) gives an excellent discussion of the problems of ancient demography generally, though his comments on survey data at pp. 65-66 n. 266 are too dismissive.

[51] See particularly John Cherry, Jack Davis, and Eleni Mantzourani, eds. *Landscape Archaeology as Long Term History: Northern Keos in the Cyclades* (Los Angeles: Monumenta Archaeologica 16, 1991) 340; Michael H. Jameson, Curtis Runnels, and Tjeerd van Andel, *A Greek Countryside: The Southern Argolid from Prehistory to the Present Day* (Stanford 1994) 544-45; John Bintliff, "Further considerations on the population of ancient Boeotia," in John Bintliff, ed. *Recent Developments in the History and Archaeology of Central Greece* (Oxford: BAR International Series 666,1997) 132-52; Susan Alcock, *Graecia Capta: The Landscapes of Roman Greece* (Cambridge 1993) 33-63, all with extensive bibliographies.

[52] Ian Morris, "Archaeology, standards of living, and Greek economic history," in Joseph Manning and Ian Morris, eds. *The Ancient Economy: Evidence and Models* (Stanford forthcoming).

pre-industrial economics,[53] and cannot be explained within Finley's framework. Text-based historians have recently begun to claim that Greek economies were larger, more complex, and more dynamic than the substantivists allowed, and the potential for an archaeological economic history focusing on growth seems enormous.[54]

CONCLUSION

I began this essay with four questions. First, I asked what kind of archaeological history we want. My answer was that cultural, economic, and social archaeological histories are all possible, and that we should pursue them; but that archaeology has little to contribute to the kind of political narrative that has long dominated the study of Greek history.

Second, I asked why we are not getting much of these kinds of archaeological history. I saw two answers here. First, the way our forefathers set up the fields of ancient history and classical archaeology in the late nineteenth century and the institutions they created make it difficult to promote such interdisciplinary work. Second, the only practical way to bring together the skills needed to do good archaeological history is to give up some of the traditional disciplinary skills. Some classicists may think that price is too high.

My third question was how we can actually do the archaeological history of Greece. I stressed focusing on longer time scales and broader regions than is normal in ancient history, and looking more at contexts of deposition than is normal in classical archaeology; but the crucial factor has to be intellectual openness. If we stop worrying about the boundaries between fields and concentrate instead on using every technique we can think of to answer the questions that we think are important, archaeological history will take care of itself.

---

[53]E.g., R.E. Lucas, Jr., "The Industrial Revolution: past and future," University of Chicago working paper. Originally presented as the 1996 Kuznets Lectures, Yale University, 1998.

[54]See Edward Cohen, *Athenian Economy and Society: A Banking Perspective* (Princeton 1992); Alain Bresson, *La cité marchande* (Paris 2000); Ian Morris, and Joseph Manning, "Introduction," (n.52).

THE FRONTIERS OF ANCIENT HISTORY: THUCYDIDES, SURVIVAL AND THE WRITING OF HISTORY

Lawrence A. Tritle

In his 1957 presidential address to the American Historical Association, entitled "The Next Assignment," William L. Langer of Harvard University suggested to his colleagues that they consider more closely psychology as a tool with which to explore their discipline. He noted the conservatism of historians who hesitated to take on new ideas, "to take flyers into the unknown, even though some of them may prove wide of the mark."[1] While there have been notable exceptions, historians today remain a conservative lot, seemingly unwilling to take those "flyers into the unknown," to explore new ideas and concepts with which to approach the past.

Langer argued that historical understanding could be enhanced "through exploitation of the concepts and findings of modern psychology."[2] Psychoanalysis and psychological doctrine in particular were stressed as a means of broadening historical understanding. Langer discussed Freudian doctrine and such concepts as repression, projection, displacement (*inter alia*), noting Freud's application of these ideas to such notable figures as da Vinci and Doestoevsky.[3] Additionally, Gustave Le

---

[1]W.L. Langer, "The Next Assignment," *AHR* 63 (1958) 284.
[2]Ibid.
[3]Among the works that Langer cited were H.W. Brosin, "A Review of the Influence of Psychoanalysis on Current Thought," in *Dynamic Psychiatry,* ed. by F. Alexander and H. Ross (Chicago 1952) 508-53, C. Kluckhohn, "The Influence of Psychiatry on Anthropology in America during the Past One Hundred Years," in *One Hundred Years of America Psychiatry,* ed. by

Bon's 1895 study of crowds and crowd psychology complemented Freud's efforts, as he investigated group experience and the notion of a collective group mind. Some historians followed these thinkers and their ideas early on. Preserved Smith's 1913 article on Luther anticipated Erik Erikson's celebrated study of the Protestant reformer by forty-five years, while Georges Lefebvre's study of the mobs and crowds in the French Revolution reflected the efforts to broaden the understanding of human reactions.[4]

The marriage, then, of psychology and history has been a long one, perhaps longer than many historians realize, and while not all may approve, it is surely here to stay. Langer's emphasis on Freud and theories of psychoanalysis reflected what was known of psychology in the 1950s. Since then, however, new dimensions to psychology lying in the area of biochemistry and neurobiology have been uncovered and explored and these have provided scholars of all disciplines with new views toward interpretations of the past. One such example is Tourette's Syndrome discussed by Oliver Sacks in his book, *An Anthropologist on Mars*. He notes that this disorder with its frightening array of obscene barks, involuntary twitches and grimaces was recorded for the first time perhaps by the second century AD physician Aretaeus of Cappadocia. As he notes, Tourette's is not a psychological disorder per se, but rather a neurobiological disorder of a hyperphysiological sort.[5] While this might be an extreme "flyer into the unknown," might the pronouncements of the Delphic Pythia be explained by something like Tourette's or a less severe disorder such as autism?[6] Along with Freud's founding principles of

---

J.K. Hall (New York 1944) 589-618, and H. Lasswell, "Impact of Psychoanalytic Thinking on the Social Sciences," in *The State of the Social Sciences*, ed. by L.D. White (Chicago 1956) 84-115.

[4]Langer (n.1) 289-90; E.H. Erikson, *Young Man Luther. A Study in Psychoanalysis and History* (New York 1958).

[5]See discussion in O. Sacks, *An Anthropologist on Mars* (New York 1995) 77-85. Fragments of Aretaeus of Cappadocia are collected in K. Hude, *CMG* 2 (1923). For additional discussion, see *TLS* November 12, 1999, where a contributor suggests that Samuel Johnson was afflicted by Tourette's.

[6]C. Sourvinou-Inwood, *s.v.* "Delphic oracle," *OCD*[3] (Oxford 1996) 445, refers to the Pythia's pronouncements as being "gibberish." See also W.

psychology, consideration of these concepts and biological forces brings entirely new perspectives on historical understanding.

Perhaps the first classicist to apply such avant-garde ideas was Friedrich Nietzsche. When Nietzsche published *The Birth of Tragedy*, he ignited a bitter feud with his former schoolmate Ulrich von Wilamowitz-Moellendorf, then perhaps the leading philologist in Germany. Von Wilamowitz-Moellendorf dismissed Nietzsche's work as *"Zukunftsphilologie"* ("future philology"), but what this really reveals is his own conservatism and attitude that what constituted classical philology could only be that which he defined.[7]

Von Wilamowitz-Moellendorf's criticisms notwithstanding, the influence of Nietzsche's ideas on classicists in his own time and afterwards has been limited. It was not long, however, before "mainstream" scholars began to explore the new disciplines, seeking ways to apply them to classical studies. In his 1949 Sather Lectures, E.R. Dodds applied then current psychological and anthropological concepts to Greek thought, subsequently publishing them as *The Greeks and the Irrational*.[8] In his introductory remarks, Dodds stated that his study was "of the successive interpretations which Greek minds placed on one particular type of human experience—a sort of experience in which nineteenth-century rationalism took little interest, but whose cultural significance is now widely recognized."[9] Here Dodds was referring to the over rationalizing of the era and to the attitudes of scholars who attempted to interpret the past from (only) a rational perspective, and to the growing realization of the usefulness of psychology and anthropology in enlarging upon our understanding of the Greeks. Since Dodd's innovative study, classicists have looked at psychology and related disciplines more broadly in order to expand their understanding of the past. One such scholar is Walter Burkert, whose study *Homo Necans* looked to

---

Burkert, *Greek Religion* (Cambridge, MA 1985) 116 and W.K.C. Guthrie, *The Greeks and Their Gods* (Boston 1950) 199-200.

[7]On the clash between Nietzsche and Wilamowitz-Moellendorf see S. Goldhill, "Modern Critical Approaches to Greek Tragedy," in *Cambridge Companion to Greek Tragedy*, ed. by P. E. Easterling (Cambridge 1997) 324-5.

[8]E.R. Dodds, *The Greeks and the Irrational* (Berkeley 1951).

[9]Ibid., vii.

aggression and human violence, ideas explored by Freud and other twentieth century scholars, to understand ancient Greek ritual and myth.[10] It has recently come to light that some scholars regarded Burkert's work much as von Wilamowitz-Moellendorf had Nietzsche's. In his review of the second edition of *Homo Necans*, Robert Parker noted that the first edition had gone unnoticed (i.e., reviewed) in *Classical Review*, *Journal of Hellenic Studies*, and *Gnomon* when it appeared. Parker suggests that finding a qualified (or interested?) reviewer may have been part of the problem. But Burkert himself revealed in 1998 that some colleagues believed that someone who could write a book like *Homo Necans* was unfit.[11] Such a response clearly reflects the conservative inclination of historians (and classicists) that Langer decried in 1957.

Since *Homo Necans* first appeared, the reception to works applying psychology, broadly defined, has been more positive, though not all scholars are pleased with such research to be sure. Burkert himself advanced to *Creation of the Sacred. Tracks of Biology in Early Religion* (1996), essentially attempting to understand ancient religion through sociobiology and biology.[12] In the recent *Cambridge Companion to Greek Tragedy*, Simon Goldhill appraised psychoanalytic criticism and tragedy, concluding "it is unlikely that the criticism of Greek tragedy can expect wholly to avoid an engagement with psychological and psychoanalytic theory."[13]

---

[10]W. Burkert, *Homo Necans. The Anthropology of Ancient Greek Sacrificial Ritual and Myth*, trans. by P. Bing (Berkeley 1983), first published as *Homo Necans* (Berlin: Walter de Gruyter & Co., 1972). At the beginning of his first chapter titled "Sacrifice, Hunting, and Funerary Rituals," Burkert notes the influence of S. Freud, *Das Unbehagen in der Kultur* (1930), in *Ges. Schriften XII* (1934) 27-114 (= *Ges. Werke XIV* (1948) 419-506). Also cited was K. Lorenz, *Das sogenennte Böse: Zur Naturgeschichte der Aggression* (Vienna 1963, 1970) and M.F.A. Montagu, *Man and Aggression* (New York 1968).

[11]R. Parker, *CR* 48 (1998) 509-10, citing W. Burkert, *Pegasus* 41 (1998) 10 (non vidi). The context of the remark is in regard to Burkert's suitability for editing a classical journal (not identified).

[12]W. Burkert, *Creation of the Sacred. Tracks* of *Biology in Early Religion* (Cambridge 1996). Similar ideas are advanced by A. Newberg, M.D., E. D'Aquili, M.D., Ph.D., and V. Rause, *Why God Won't Go Away. Brain Science and the Biology of Belief* (New York 2001).

[13]Goldhill, (n. 7) 343.

Yet the role of psychology and its application by historians is hardly a new story. Historians, Langer noted, beginning with Thucydides "have habitually thought of themselves as psychologists in their own right."[14] He added, however, that historians while on the one hand, freely indulging in psychological interpretation, have feared psychological doctrine as too biological and deterministic, and have been too reluctant to deal with unconscious motives and irrational forces. Historians, for these reasons, have clung "to the methods of historicism, restricting themselves to recorded facts and to strictly rational motivation."[15]

Such attitudes, however, ignore the realities of modern science, including the connection between biology (broadly defined) and psychology that every day finds more links.[16] Yet what some fail to consider is that human beings can show great independence of action even when exposed to similar challenges, whether in the laboratory or in real life. Moreover, historians' concern that psychological doctrine is too deterministic is actually shared by biologists and scientists. In the preface to *Aggression and Violence*, David M. Stoff and Robert B. Cairns identify several "myths" concerning the biology of aggression and violence. Their first myth is that "violence can be reduced to and explained on the basis of disordered biological processes." They go on to say that "investigators are demonstrating the wide array of circumstances in which social structure and social behavior have a direct influence on physiological and hormonal processes."[17] Psychology, then, only provides an additional

---

[14]Langer (n. 1) 288.

[15]Ibid.

[16]Two eminently readable works that introduce the layman to the nature of biology and psychology are by Stanford biochemist and MacArthur fellow Robert Sapolsky: *Why Zebras Don't Get Ulcers. An Updated Guide to Stress, Stress-Related Diseases, and Coping* (New York 1994, 1998) and *The Trouble with Testosterone and Other Essays on the Biology of the Human Predicament* (New York 1997). Both are highly recommended. Sapolsky's laboratory and field work greatly elaborate Erich Fromm, *The Anatomy of Human Destructiveness* (New York 1973), who called attention to the connections between pyschology and man's behavior but without the physiological element that is today so commonplace.

[17]D.M. Stoff and R.B. Cairns, edd., *Aggression and Violence: Genetic, Neurobiological, and Biosocial Perspectives* (Mahwah, NJ 1996) xiii.

tool—not the only tool—with which the historian may interpret the past.

Walter Burkert explored the nature of violence in relation to Greek ritual and myth and in posing new questions to an old topic surely enriched our understanding of it. Though Thucydides did not understand human psychology as we do today, he had experience with men, including experience in violent situations. Here he was able to observe the human experience with violence with what we today can see as the intersection of biology and psychology. What is offered here then is an interpretation of Thucydides' work that considers the modern psychological perspective: the nature of violence and how the human experience with violence influences the survivor.[18]

ON THUCYDIDES, SURVIVAL AND THE WRITING OF HISTORY

Much has been written of Thucydides, but the view stressed here is that from the perspective of a survivor of violence and seeks to understand how that experience influenced his *History*. Surviving violent acts, the sort that all too routinely occur in war, should not be imagined as a simple process, the sort of thing that can be left in the past as life moves on. The American Psychiatric Association in its 1987 *Diagnostic and Statistical Manual of Psychiatric Disorders* (i.e., the *DSM* III-R) defined a traumatic event as "outside the usual range of experience." As Judith Herman notes, however, traumatic events are really extraordinary because they "overwhelm the ordinary human adaptations to life."[19]

Judith Herman's important study *Trauma and Recovery* effectively and clearly relates the consequences of the ordinary human response to danger, showing that it is "a complex, integrated system of reactions, encompassing both body and

---

[18]The interpretation of the nature of violence discussed here follows the biological parameters discussed above. Readers might be interested in another more religious and philosophic discourse on violence, ideas developed by René Girard. For discussion see G. Bailie, *Violence Unveiled. Humanity at the Crossroads* (New York 1995).

[19]American Psychiatric Association, *Diagnostic and Statistical Manual of Psychiatric Disorder,* 3rd ed. (=*DSM*-III-R) (Washington D.C. 1987) 236; J. Herman, M.D., *Trauma and Recovery* (New York 1992) 33.

mind."[20] Threats arouse the sympathetic nervous system which releases combinations of neurohormones secreted by the adrenal gland, including adrenaline and a group of steroids known as glucocorticoids, that allow humans to cope with stressful situations.[21] Neither Achilles nor Hector, Jonathan Shay in *Achilles in Vietnam* notes, "could have remained alive for more than thirty seconds in the absence of cortisol (i.e., the chemical that enables humans to withstand stress).[22] Such a modern and scientific analysis might seem out of place in analyzing the events of the ancient world, but there is little doubt that "ancient" Greeks responded to stress in the same way as "modern" Americans. At the battle of Marathon, the Athenian soldier Epizelus was fighting away when he saw the man next to him cut down. The next thing he remembered was a giant warrior, so tall that his beard covered Epizelus' shield. Then, in an instance, he went blind and never saw the light of day again.[23] Numerous cases of "hysterical blindness" may be cited in modern history, ranging from World War II veterans filmed in John Huston's 1946 film *Let There Be Light* to Cambodian women refugees living today in Long Beach, California.[24]

Human reactions to stress then are greatly similar and cut across time and culture. It should not be thought, however, that after the threat passes, the body returns to its "normal" state. In

---

[20]Herman, ibid., 35. In addition to Herman's important study, see also E. Scarry, *The Body in Pain. The Making and Unmaking of the World* (New York 1985).

[21]Sapolsky (n. 14, 1997) 120-1.

[22]J. Shay, M.D., Ph.D., *Achilles in Vietnam. Combat Trauma and the Undoing of Character* (New York 1994) 92.

[23]Hdt. 6.117-2-3, see the discussion in L.A. Tritle, *From Melos to My Lai. War and Survival* (London 2000) 63-4. Another case of "hysterical blindness" may be that of the Spartan Eurytes who became blind at Thermopylae in 480 and was led to the final battle there by his helot servant (Hdt. 7. 232).

[24]See Tritle, ibid., 8, n. 16 for reference to the Cambodian women. For definition and discussion of hysterical blindness see E.A. Weinstein, M.D., "Conversion Disorders," in R. Zajtchuk, ed., *Textbook of Military Medicine*, 4 pts. (Falls Church, Virginia 1994-5) I, 4, 383-407; Jonathan Shay agrees with the diagnosis of Epizelus' blindness offered here (e-mail communication, June 28, 1999). The Hanks-Spielberg HBO mini-series of fall 2001, *Band of Brothers*, depicted a case of hysterical blindness in its third episode, the case of American soldier Albert Blithe.

fact, "traumatized people feel and act as though their nervous systems have been disconnected from the present," and they continue to react to the trauma.[25] This reaction expresses itself in the form of hyperarousal, intrusion and constriction, all symptoms of what is today known as post-traumatic stress disorder (PTSD). Full discussion of these symptoms is beyond the scope of this essay, but a few brief definitions may be offered. Hyperarousal is defined as the persistent expectation of danger; intrusion is the "indelible" imprint of the traumatic moment in which traumatized people relive the event as if it were continually recurring; while constriction is the numbing of body and mind, seen by some as way for the psyche to keep "traumatic memories out of normal consciousness, allowing only a fragment of the memory to emerge as an intrusive symptom".[26]

For those caught in the vicious cycle of war, the consequences of violence in turn unleash the thirst for revenge. This Jonathan Shay has defined as one of the attributes of the berserk warrior who fights with no regard for his own life, determined only to make others pay for the loss of friends. Revenge, Shay notes, "denies helplessness, keeps faith with the dead, and affirms that there is still justice in the world, even if this is manifested only in the survivor's random vengeance."[27] Revenge or payback is a psychological response to trauma that follows from natural biochemical and physiological changes.

Human chemistry then dictates the predictable range of responses which culture will follow rather than guide. In making my case I shall draw on the events and the circumstances of another violent conflict, one more recent than Thucydides' war—Vietnam. It might seem that these conflicts have little in common—after all one happened two thousand years ago, the other only thirty. In the world-view of many of today's students and probably many people generally, both events are equally remote. Yet in studying Thucydides and his account of the Peloponnesian War, one can find a number of scholars who have seen a similarity of happenings: the horror of violence in late fifth century Greece in any number of places evokes comparison with Vietnam. The violence and circumstances of both influenced the language used to relate

---

[25]Herman, ibid., 35.

[26]Ibid. See further Herman, 35-47 for discussion of these three conditions.

[27]Shay (n. 22) 89-90.

events. Those familiar with Thucydides recall only too well his remarks on the *stasis* of Corcyra: "To fit in with the change of events, words too had to change their usual meanings" (Thuc. 3.82.2). There is little separating this description of the changes and contortions inflicted on language amid violence and the famous statement of a US Army officer at Ben Tre, Vietnam in 1968: "It became necessary to destroy the town to save it."

THUCYDIDES THE SURVIVOR

In his famous study *The Idea of History*, R.G. Collingwood observed that "the style of Herodotus is easy, spontaneous, convincing. That of Thucydides is harsh, artificial, repellant. In reading Thucydides I ask myself, 'What is the matter with the man, that he writes like that?' I answer: he has a bad conscience. He is trying to justify himself for writing history at all by turning it into something that is not history."[28] Collingwood then proceeded to critique Thucydides on the grounds that he wrote psychological history, which in his view was not history at all. A full exploration of Collingwood's view could easily be a paper in itself. Allow me to remark only that Collingwood's argument overlooks what it is that the historian must often do, i.e., "venture into the realm of psychology" in order to explain the motives and actions of men and societies.[29] Collingwood seems not to have realized it, but he actually stumbled on to a key factor explaining Thucydides' style of writing history: namely, that experiences in Thucydides' life influenced his language and style in the *History*. What Collingwood and others studying Thucydides have not appreciated is his experience with the violence of the Peloponnesian War and how this would explain the language of violence that he brought to his work.

That Thucydides served as *strategos* or general in the Peloponnesian War is well known. So too his self-imposed exile in the war's eighth year, a decision taken to avoid the wrath of his fellow Athenians, following his loss of the strategic town of Amphipolis in the northern Aegean to the Spartans. What has remained unappreciated is that Thucydides had already spent six years, 431-424, fighting in the great war with Sparta. This

---

[28]R.G. Collingwood, *The Idea of History* (Oxford 1946) 29.
[29]A. Marwick, *The Nature of History* (New York 1962) 141, and noted too by Langer (n. 1) 286.

experience with violence, not to mention what he had experienced before the war erupted, left him a survivor who—as in the cases of other survivors of violence—had an outlook on events different from those not so experienced. An example of this is evident in his account of the Spartan survivor of Sphacteria taunted by an Athenian ally who asked if the "real" Spartans had died in that battle. The Spartan replied that "it would be some arrow that could pick out the brave man" (Thuc. 4.40.2). This laconic statement has attracted some scholarly attention and effort to interpret it. I would agree generally with Gomme and Hornblower who place it in a context of bravery amid indiscriminate death. Yet the profundity of this remark has remained unappreciated and Hornblower's description of it as a "joke" simply misses the mark.

The warrior's retort reflects in fact the psychic trauma of a survivor of catastrophe who can only relate events in profound and cryptic fashion. Let me provide a comparable example from Vietnam. In Michael Herr's riveting and powerful memoir *Dispatches* appears his account of an encounter with an apparently psychotic LURP (i.e., Long Range Reconnaissance Patrol, sometimes abbreviated LRRP). This man had clearly seen too much battle—now in his third tour in Vietnam, he was the only survivor from his platoon destroyed in the Ia Drang battle of 1965, and subsequently of his Special Forces team, also all killed but him. Herr relates how he was unable to function at home in "the World," and passed the time by aiming a rifle out of the window of his parents' home, leading people and cars as they passed. His parents were, as he himself admitted, "real uptight" about this! But more powerful was the story he told Herr: "Patrol went up the mountain. One man came back. He died before he could tell us what happened." Herr commented that he waited for the ending, the "moral," of the story. When nothing further was offered he asked, "What happened." The LURP "just looked at me like he felt sorry for me, fucked if he'd waste time telling stories to anyone as dumb as I was."[30]

---

[30]M. Herr, *Dispatches* (New York 1978) 6-7. Similar statements are in evidence from other conflicts: the survivor of Iwo Jima asked by his children what it had been like, only to hear that "it was tough;" or Confederate Captain Praxiteles Swan on Gettysburg: "We all went up to Gettysburg, the

Thucydides' Spartan survivor of Sphacteria, Michael Herr's LURP, and other survivors of violence are united in their difficulty in relating events, especially traumatic events, that they have experienced. In order for the survivor to cope with that trauma, the event must be reflected on obliquely rather than directly. There may also be a perceived need to establish a barrier between the participant and non-participant because many survivors believe that those who have not experienced the trauma can not really understand it when it is related.[31] Consequently, there arises a need to find or create a new language and a new method to relate these traumatic events. In the case of Thucydides what emerged was his account of the Peloponnesian War, what we today call his *History*, but what may also be seen as a work inspired to a certain extent by a close experience with violence.

Like so many other things associated with violence, language also changes as a result of the situations and the contexts to which it is applied. This was noted by Thucydides when he wrote his account of the Peloponnesian War.[32] As he lived through the conflict he recorded, he had the opportunity to reflect on the events and on the nuances of their implications and consequences. This is revealed in the passage cited above, a part of his analysis of the violence that destroyed the *polis* of Corcyra of its humanity and community as a result of civil strife that erupted in 427 BC. Thucydides plainly states that the events literally created a new language, a language of violence in which words changed or acquired new meanings in order to conform with the realities brought by violence induced change. Much the same thing occurred in Vietnam, where as Michael Herr relates

> All in-country briefings, at whatever levels, came to sound like a naming of the Parts, and the language was used as a cosmetic, but one that diminished the beauty. Since most of the journalism from the war was framed in that language or proceeded from the view of the war which those terms implied, it would be as impossible to know what

---

summer of '63: and some of us came back from there: and that's all except the details."

[31] See Tritle (n. 23) 67-71 for discussion.

[32] See the discussion below.

Vietnam looked like from reading most newspaper stories as it would be to know how it smelled.[33]

Michael Herr and Thucydides saw that violence had a way of influencing language as well as the thoughts of those who were exposed to it. It might be argued that any sort of a comparison between these two authors ignores some very real differences. One was a newsman, a journalist who wrote "popular" stories about a nasty little war, while the other was an historian who recorded the events of a "great" and significant conflict. Such distinctions as these are plainly superficial and ignore the attempt at understanding complex events that both authors made. Moreover, both Thucydides and Herr make clear that violence shaped the minds and words of those who were confronted by it, whether as observers or as participants, and this too brings them together. What they show us then in much the same way is the historiography, the literature and language of violence.

VIOLENCE AND LANGUAGE

But war is a violent teacher; in depriving them of the power of easily satisfying their daily wants, it brings most people's minds down to the level of their actual circumstances.

Thuc. 3.82.3

When Thucydides wrote "war is a violent teacher," he spoke from experience and not merely as an observer of the greatest and most violent war ever fought by the Greeks.[34] His military service attests further the active role he played: he was a witness to the violence that increasingly characterized the prolonged conflict that, as he remarks, brought people down to the level of their circumstances. As Aeschylus before him, Thucydides was a survivor of war's violence, an experience that heightened his awareness to the toll of violence.[35] What he learned of events, the massacres at places like Plataea and Mitylene in 427 and

---

[33]Herr (n. 30) 92-3.

[34]Thuc. 1.1 refers to the war as the greatest ever fought by the Greeks. This and other passages (e.g., 3.82, 7.30) suggest that Thucydides lived through the Peloponnesian War and then was revising the entire history when he died (i.e., the *History* ends abruptly in 411/10). For more detailed treatment see S. Hornblower, *Thucydides* (Baltimore 1987) 136-54.

[35]Discussed in Tritle (n. 23) 159-60, 43, 11.

other places throughout the war, influenced his work. But the horrors that occurred in Corcyra in 427 gave new meaning to the realities of war and violence. This necessitated a new language of violence that Thucydides created, inspired by untold reports of atrocities.

Corcyra was perhaps the flashpoint that ignited the Peloponnesian War in 431. A powerful and unattached maritime state off the western coast of Greece, Corcyra entered into a defensive alliance with Athens after becoming embroiled in a bitter dispute with Corinth, her much hated mother city.[36] Several naval engagements resulted in the capture and detention of a large number of Corcyraeans in Corinth. The Corinthians won a number of these over to their side and then released them home with the idea that they would break the Corcyraean alliance with Athens.[37] This Corinthian ploy took shape in 427 when these men returned home and quickly challenged the democratic, pro-Athenian party led by Peithias.[38] A prosecution for subversion failed to topple Peithias, who retaliated against five of his opponents with charges of sacrilege. His plans not only miscarried but worse: the opposition attacked him and his political allies in council chambers and killed over sixty of them with knives in a particularly brutal scene. Within a short time Corcyra was in an uproar as vicious street fighting erupted between democrats and conservatives. Thucydides relates how even women joined in, hurling down roof tiles and "standing up to the din of battle with courage beyond their sex."[39]

The presence of allies, Athenians for the democrats and Peloponnesians and Spartans for the conservatives,

---

[36]Thuc. 1.24-55. The dispute between Corcyra and Corinth broke out when a third city, Epidamnus located on the Adriatic coast, appealed to Corinth for aid after Corcyra had refused help in fending off native attacks from the interior. The Corcyraeans were angered at this Corinthian intrusion into their backyard and so went to war. On the enmity between Corcyra and Corinth see, e.g., J.B. Salmon, *Wealthy Corinth. A History of the City to 338 BC* (Oxford 1989).

[37]Corinth had a long withstanding grudge with Athens dating back some twenty years to a particularly nasty Athenian massacre of a group of Corinthian soldiers. See Thuc. 1.103, 106.

[38]Thuc. 3.71-2.

[39]Thuc. 3.75.1. He notes that these were "democratic" women, but one wonders if the "conservative" women would stand idly by amid all the violence.

compounded the violence and inflamed the passions on both sides. This rapidly growing community rupture then exploded into a seven-day paroxysm of violence. The democrats were able to gain the upper hand and the resulting violence, as Thucydides relates, must have been horrific. Men were killed under pretense of trials and truces; asylum seekers in temples committed suicide rather than be killed by their enemies. Charges of conspiracy became mere ruses to kill those hated on personal grounds or on account of holding debts. It became worse and soon

> there was death in every shape and form. As it usually happens in such situations, people went to every extreme and beyond it. There were fathers who killed their sons; men were dragged from the temples or butchered on the very altars.[40]

Thucydides' narration and description of the savage encounter in Corcyra is but a prelude to his much deeper psychological analysis. He begins with the reference to how the revolution in Corcyra was but the first of many, a statement that tells us that he indeed saw the end of the war that enabled him to reach such conclusions as this. He notes the divisions into pro-Athenian and pro-Spartan factions in the Greek cities and how these became regular political features. His observations then take a broader analytical look at human nature, arguing that the tragedies that occurred at Corcyra will always happen "while human nature is what it is, though there may be different degrees of savagery, and, as different circumstances arise, the general rules will admit of some variety."[41]

This explanation some modern readers will find objectionable, owing to what they perceive as Thucydides' appeal to "human nature," particularly the fixed notion he suggests. Such criticism, however, fails to recognize just what prompted him to reach this conclusion. In two places in his analysis he refers to revenge. 3.82.1 refers to the extravagant plans that were made for seizing power and of the "unheard of atrocities in revenge" that accompanied them. At 3.82.3, he states that "revenge was more important than self-preservation." Thucydides' reference to the dominance of revenge, then, points

---

[40]Thuc. 3.81.4. It is interesting to note that the Athenian commander and his squadron of ships were present while this slaughter took place, providing perhaps moral and material support.

[41]Thuc. 3.81.5.

to the very real presence of trauma and its consequences influencing the actions of the Corcyraeans and those other Greeks who also became ensnared in the savage cycle of violence. As noted above, Jonathan Shay and other psychiatrists have argued that revenge is a psychological response to trauma that follows from natural biochemical and psychological changes.

The violence unleashed by the civil war in Corcyra, the payback that led to the "unheard of atrocities" that Thucydides alludes to, produced the deterioration of moral values that could allow people to transgress religious scruples and kill on sacred ground and worse. This deterioration in morals is reflected also in his language and how "to fit in with the change of events, words too, had to change their usual meanings." In analyzing the civil strife in Corcyra, Thucydides writes that "irrational recklessness" became "courageous commitment," "hesitation" and concern for the future was seen as cowardice, while "senseless anger" defined a true man and the intriguer who succeeded was intelligent yes, but not nearly so as one who detected a plot. The casual reader of Thucydides might well pass over these definitions and word changes without realizing the forces that have shaped these views. But Thucydides' experience with the violence of war, informed too by the cultural experimentation of the Greek Enlightenment, may be illuminated by a comparable violent experience, that of Vietnam.

To ignore the contortion of language that took place in Vietnam is to miss an essential dimension of that "Experience." The first level of word change is that which occurs on the superficial level, i.e., terms that are descriptive of violence, so much so that they can only be expressed with bitter sarcasm. Terms like "crispy critters" to describe napalm casualties and dead, or a detached limb as the result of "response-to-impact" fall into this category.[42] Michael Herr mentions soldiers of the 173rd Airborne Brigade referring to the "KIA [Killed in Action] Travel Bureau," when referring to the processing home of the bodies of their dead buddies. Much more sinister, however, is "payback," the term that evolved to describe the revenge visited on the enemy. Perhaps the best definition of this is to be found in Gustav Hasford's *The Short Timers*, the work that became

---

[42]Herr (n. 30) 18. The term "crispy critters" began c. 1967/8 and is a term often found in Vietnam writings.

the Stanley Kubrick film *Full Metal Jacket*. Here Hasford's character "Animal Mother" gives a brutally lucid statement of what motivated combat soldiers in Vietnam.

> You think we waste gooks for *free*dom? Don't kid yourself; this is slaughter....Yeah, you better believe we zap zipperheads. They waste our bros and we cut them a big piece of payback. And payback is a motherfucker.[43]

Payback is simply revenge, which as Thucydides and Hasford both show, inflicts "unheard-of atrocities" that themselves induce payback in an unending cycle of violence.[44]

But perhaps the most telling of all the word changes to come out of Vietnam is the paradoxical "It don't mean nothin." This phrase can be found in the literary works of Vietnam veterans as well as the discussions of their therapists and counselors. Jonathan Shay refers to it as "the Vietnam combat soldiers' mantra, spread out to engulf everything valued or wanted, every person, loyalty, and commitment."[45] Vietnam veteran and author William Broyles refers to it as meaning "everything, it means too much. Language overload."[46] Taken together both definitions explain what processes are at work in creating such language. An experience so brutal and extreme that it lies outside normative language and represents an event that runs counter to every principle, value and right one has been taught. To cope with this event, then, language adapts and so changes to conform with the transformed reality that the survivor of that event has experienced.[47]

It is in this context that Thucydides' new definition of violence should be understood. He states that daringly wild

---

[43]G. Hasford, *The Short-Timers* (New York 1979) 136.

[44]It is of some interest to note that payback, as other words from the Vietnam experience, have become idiomatic in contemporary American English colloquial speech.

[45]Shay (n. 22) 38.

[46]F. Broyles, "Why Men Love War," in W. Capps, ed., *The Vietnam Reader* (New York 1991) 75.

[47]See J. Wilson, "The Customary Meanings of Words were Changed—or Were They? A Note on Thucydides 3.82.4," *CQ* 32 (1982): 18-20, for a different view. Wilson argues that the "words" did not change their meaning as much as acquired new meanings as situations themselves changed. But does this not mean that the words acquired new connotations—essentially meanings?

aggression (*tolma...alogistos*) was now seen as brotherly commitment (*philetairos enomiste*). Concern for the future (*mellesis...promethes*) was cowardice (*deila euprepes*), while moderation, one of the great Greek virtues handed down from Apollo (i.e., "the golden mean"), *to...sophron*, had become unmanliness, or within the Greek scheme of things, womanly. The circumspect or careful individual (*to pros pan xuneton*) was really the inactive one (*epi pan argon*), and the violent man (*ho chalapainon*) was always trustworthy (*pistos*) and anyone who spoke against him was suspect (*hypoptos*).

Thucydides' definitions reflect his survivor's instincts to see things in a different way than the non-survivor and with a sarcastic and bitter edge. Without this sarcasm and bitter irony, as in the aforementioned "crispy critters," or in the designation of Vietnamese dead as "believers,"[48] it is difficult to understand how Thucydides could imagine the moderate man, for example, as womanly. From the bitter standpoint of the survivor, however, the formation of such words and the ideas they represent becomes comprehensible.

Another factor that influenced Thucydides here was the intellectual development current in Athens when he wrote, the so-called "Greek Enlightenment." This was one of the great intellectual "booms" of all time and saw the flowering of drama, both tragedy and comedy, philosophy with the likes of Socrates and the Sophists, rhetoric and history, the latter with Thucydides. This was a great mixing of ideas and it comes as no surprise to see Thucydides experimenting with various ideas and approaches in his "inquiry" or history of the war between Athens and Sparta. It is in this context that his experimentation with language and word changes, his use of the dialogue form later made famous by Plato, is to be placed. His experiences in war, however, predisposed him to interpret these developments differently.

The impact of these experiences can be seen by way of contrast with Herodotus, his great predecessor in the birth of historical writing. Herodotus wrote in the generation before Thucydides when the era of the Enlightenment was just underway. Yet his writing does not show the same sort of language experimentation and contortion as Thucydides, and the explanation may well rest in the differences in their experiences: Herodotus the exiled traveler and historian laureate

---

[48]Herr (n. 30) 42.

of Athens, and Thucydides the failed and exiled commander turned historian. It was noted above that Aeschylus, a survivor of another violent conflict, emerged from that experience and became a cultural leader in the development of making drama the art form and the teacher of the Greeks that we associate with it in the modern world. In much the same way Thucydides, another survivor, also put his experiences, reactions and survivor mentality into his work. In doing so he too would become influential in the formation of the emerging genre of historical writing.

The intellectual climate in which Thucydides composed his history is not to be discounted here, or the survivor experience made into the single greatest factor in his formation as a writer and a thinker. Yet it remains that Thucydides was impressed by the horrors of war he saw and had reported to him. One such case was the destruction of the city of Mycalessus in central Greece in 413. Here Thracian mercenaries under Athenian command attacked an unsuspecting and relatively obscure place and destroyed it. Thucydides writes

> The Thracians burst into Mycalessus, sacked the houses and temples, and butchered the inhabitants, sparing neither the young nor the old, but methodically killing everyone they met, women and children alike, and even the farm animals and every living thing they saw....Among other things, they broke into a boy's school, the largest of the place, into which the children had just entered, and killed every one of them.[49]

The scene that Thucydides evokes here is what any modern reader of the My Lai massacre would see in the photographs taken there—animals killed, women and children cut down wherever encountered. In creating this portrait Thucydides clearly intends this incident to serve an exemplary fashion, to convey the horror of the war he served in and lived through. This can be seen in the details of the slaughter in the cited passage, but other points can be added. Among these is the use of the verb *katakoptein*, to butcher, a verb that is close in meaning to *kreokopein*, to butcher or literally, "cut meat." Thucydides also stresses the non-combatant casualties, mentioning the killing of women once and that of children

---

[49]Thuc. 7.29-30. For a recent discussion see T.J. Quinn, "Thucydides and the Massacre at Mycalessus," *Mnemosyne* 1995, 571-3.

twice.[50] As in the discussion of Corcyra and how it served as a paradigm for revolutionary violence, it appears that Thucydides took Mycalessus as paradigmatic for what befell a town taken by storm. This seems evident in his closing sentence, "Mycalessus lost a considerable part of its population. It was a small city, but in the disaster just described its peoples suffered calamities as pitiable as any which took place during the war."[51]

The slaughter of the innocents at Mycalessus, however, was matched by a growing ferocity on the battlefield, events that also shaped Thucydides' writing in an even more personal way. Accounts of these battles might well have evoked in him the emotions of Odysseus who, on hearing of the tale of Troy, took a great cloak

dyed in sea-purple, drew it over his head and veiled his fine features, shamed for tears running down his face.[52]

Odysseus' reaction is mirrored by that of eighty year old World War II veteran Ralph Berke, who after seeing *Saving Private Ryan* said," 'I hope I don't have nightmares again,' wiping away the tears."[53] Thucydides' description of what occurred on the battlefields of the Peloponnesian War reveal too the increase in the war's bloody toll. At the battle of Delium in 424, Thucydides tells of the Thespians, fighting against the Athenians, who were surrounded and cut down. Also killed though were a number of Athenians, struck down by their own men who did not recognize them—an example of "friendly fire" in the ancient world.[54] What Thucydides omits here is that it is not so much that these Athenians were killed by accident, as they were killed on account of the terror and confusion of battle. Ron Kovic tells of killing another Marine in much the same way in Vietnam: "I think I might have killed the corporal.... It was very confusing. It was hard to tell what was happening."[55]

Even more chilling, however, is Thucydides' account of the slaughter of the Athenian army retreating from its failed effort

---

[50]Thuc. 7.29.3 (women and children), 7.29.5 (attack and slaughter at the boy's school).

[51]Thuc. 7.30.3.

[52]Hom. *Od.* 8.84-6.

[53]Reported in the *Los Angeles Times*, July 27, 1998, p. F10.

[54]Thuc. 4.96.3, who uses *katakoptein*, to butcher, in describing how the Thespians were cut down.

[55]R. Kovic, *Born on the Fourth of July* (New York 1976) 193.

to capture Syracuse in 413. What began as an orderly withdrawal degenerated into a rout with the Syracusans and their Peloponnesian allies ripping into the battered Athenians again and again. Exhausted and near mad from thirst, the Athenians plunged in utter confusion into the Assinarus River where they were destroyed. Thucydides describes how

> the Syracusans [hurled] missiles down at the Athenians as they were drinking thirstily.... And the Peloponnesians descended and did the most butchery when they were in the river. The water immediately turned foul but was drunk just as much as when full of blood along with the mud but fought over by most of them.[56]

Thucydides' account of this slaughter is marked by the language of terror that conveys vividly what befell the Athenians. The verb he used to describe the Peloponnesian massacre of the Athenians is *sphagein*, which is used to describe sacrificial slaughter as in the cutting of throats, i.e., a particularly bloody act. Elsewhere he uses a participal form of *phoneuein*, another strong word for slaughter or the taking of life. Taken together these passages relate war on the battlefield as no less violent than what Thucydides describes in the case of the revolutions that wracked Corcyra and so many other places in the Greek world. Study of Thucydides and his language of violence alongside that of Michael Herr (and other Vietnam era writers) demonstrates convincingly that the violence encountered on the battlefields carried over into the language of those who were caught up in it.

CONCLUSION

It may be thought that the foregoing discussion reflects only a dialogue between past and present, an example of the interaction between contemporary events and issues and the interpretation of classical texts.[57] There is, of course, some truth to this as the study of history is always seen in light of the

---

[56]Thuc. 7.84.2-5.

[57]Suggested to me by S. Burnstein in a private communication, February 2, 2000, referring e.g. to A.G. Woodhouse, *Thucydides and the Nature of Power*, Martin Classical Lectures, vol. 24 (Cambridge 1970). Woodhouse in fact referred to Vietnam in several instances (pp. 22-3, 154-6), particularly the use of power by which the Athenians attempted to intimidate the Melians in 415 BC.

present. Yet to remain content with only this explanation misses some larger issues.

Langer's argument that historians should look to psychology and by extension other disciplines for tools of interpreting the past remains as valid today as in 1957 and perhaps more so. Historians need to think "outside the box" and to take account of the discoveries and findings of other disciplines that might be of assistance to them. This is not to claim that psychology and human physiology offer the only valid tool of interpretation—again it is helpful to remember that the scientists tell us this, that there are multiple factors involved in explaining behavior. Too seldom, however, are these taken advantage of and this only deprives the historian of a potentially useful tool of historical investigation. In short, historians should not fear psychology as the child fears the night.

It may also be argued that consideration of the psychological imperative argues for a certain constancy of both human nature and text. There will be undoubtedly resistance to such a notion, but as Jonathan Shay notes, "we are one species, sharing a common physiology and a common disposition to acquire culture." Shay goes on to add that this idea is not "culturally relative" and this view, I would argue, is supported by the same reactions to stress in ancient Greeks, and modern Americans and Cambodians.[58] An understanding of the human condition, both its physiology and psychology, enables the historian to interpret more fully how people react to the events and world around them. In much the same way, the texts that the historian reads and interprets may be seen to have a certain meaning in a particular time. The implications of this for postmodern thought—the notion that a text can mean whatever one wants it to—can be seen as a view that lacks a full understanding of the human author of that text.[59]

[58]Shay (n. 22) 208.

[59]I would like to thank both Stanley Burstein and Carol Thomas for their interest and suggestions in this discussion, as also their moral support over the course of the last year—and that of so many members of this Association as well.

ABOUT THE AUTHORS

Stanley M. Burstein is Professor of Ancient History and Chair of the History Department at California State University, Los Angeles, where he has taught since 1968. He was educated at the University of California, Los Angeles, receiving his Ph.D. in 1972. A long-time member of the Association of Ancient Historians, he has served as its Secretary-Treasurer and President. His area of research is Hellenistic history with particular emphasis on Greco-Roman Egypt and its relations with its African neighbors. Among his recent books are: *Agatharchides of Cnidus, On the Erythraean Sea* (London, 1989); *Graeco-Africana: Studies in the History of Greek Relations with Egypt and Nubia* (New Rochelle, 1995); *Ancient African Civilizations: Kush and Axum* (Princeton, 1998); *Ancient Greece: A Political, Social, and Cultural History* (with W. Donlan, S.B. Pomeroy, and J.T. Roberts [New York, 1999]); and *Land of Enchanters: Egyptian Short Stories from the Earliest Times to the Present Day* (with Bernard Lewis [Princeton, 2001]).

Nancy Demand recently retired as Professor of Greek History at Indiana University at Bloomington, where she taught after previous appointments at Trenton State College and Ohio State University. She was educated at the University of Pennsylvania, receiving a Ph.D. in Philosophy in 1965 and Bryn Mawr, receiving a Ph.D. in Greek in 1978. Her areas of research are the early history of the *polis*, the history of the Greek family, and ancient medicine. Her books include: *Thebes in the Fifth Century: Heracles Resurgent* (London, 1982), *Urban Relocation in Archaic and Classical Greece* (Norman, 1990), *Birth Death and Motherhood in Classical Greece* (Baltimore, 1994), and *A History of Ancient Greece* (New York, 1996).

Ian Morris is Jean and Rebecca Willard Professor of Ancient History and Archaeology at Stanford University, where he has taught since 1995. He came to Stanford from the University of Chicago, where he was an Assistant and Associate Professor in the Departments of History and Classics at the University of Chicago. He was educated at Cambridge University. He received his Ph.D. in 1985 and was a Research Fellow at Jesus College before coming to the United States. His research interests are the social, economic, and cultural history of ancient Greece, the Mediterranean Iron Age, and archaeological theory and practice. He is currently publishing the Iron Age deposits from Lerna; and is working on a study of manhood, equality, and democracy in Iron Age Greece to be published by Oxford University Press. His books include: *Burial and Ancient Society* (Cambridge, 1987), *Death-Ritual and Social Structure in Classical Antiquity* (Cambridge, 1992), *Classical Greece: Ancient Histories and Modern Archaeologies* (Cambridge 1994), *A New Companion to Homer* (with Barry Powell [Leiden, 1997]), and *Archaeology as Cultural History: Words and Things in Iron Age Greece* (Oxford, 2000).

Lawrence A. Tritle is Professor of Greek History at Loyola-Marymount University, where he has taught since 1978. He was educated at the University of California, Los Angeles, the University of South Florida, and the University of Chicago, receiving his Ph.D. in 1978. He has served as President of the International Plutarch Society and Co-Chairman of the Friends of Ancient History, and is currently co-editor of the *Ancient History Bulletin*. His research areas are Greek and Balkan history and contemporary issues and the classics. His books include: *Phocion the Good* (London, 1988), *The Greek World in the Fourth Century BC: From the Fall of the Athenian Empire to the Successors of Alexander* (London, 1997), *Balkan Currents: Studies in the History, Culture and Society of a Divided Land* (Claremont, 1998), *Text and Tradition. Studies in Greek History and Historiography in Honor of Mortimer Chambers* (with R. Mellor [Claremont, 1999]), and *From Melos to My Lai. War and Survival* (London 2000).